buying the **dragon's teeth**

buying the **dragon's teeth**

How Your Money Empowers a Cruel and Dangerous Communist Regime in China, and Undermines Labor, Industry and Freedom Worldwide

jamyang norbu

BLUEJAY BOOKS

An imprint of Srishti Publishers & Distributors
New Delhi & Calcutta

BLUEJAY BOOKS
An imprint of Srishti Publishers & Distributors
64-A, Adhchini
Sri Aurobindo Marg
New Delhi 110 017
srishtipublishers@yahoo.com

First published by High Asia Press, New York, 2004
This edition published by BLUEJAY BOOKS, 2005
in association with High Asia Press, U.S.A.

Editor : Lisa S. Keary

Cover and Interior Design: Phustok Jorhen

ISBN 81-88575-56-9

Printed and bound in India

The Colchian king Ætes consented to give up the golden fleece if Jason would yoke to the plough two fire-breathing bulls with brazen feet and sow the teeth of the dragon which Cadmus had slain, and from which it was well known that a crop of armed men would spring up, who would turn their weapons against their producer.

... Jason next proceeded to sow the dragon's teeth and plough them in. And soon the crop of armed men sprang up, and, wonderful to relate! No sooner had they reached the surface than they began to brandish their weapons and rush upon Jason.

— Thomas Bulfinch, *The Age of Fable or Stories of Gods and Heroes*

Contents

Introduction

(to the 2004 edition)

It is in the spirit of the Chinese saying: "even the palest ink is better than the strongest memory" that this revised, renamed and extensively extended edition of the original pamphlet *Made in China* has been put together. For, regrettably, human memory is far from strong when it comes to remembering China's crimes against humanity,* even when they are ongoing, as they always are, and when the profit motive somehow becomes involved in the process, as it usually does.

Of course, articles and reports on China's harvesting of transplant organs of executed prisoners, religious persecution, mass executions, slave labor camps and nationwide forced abortions do appear in newspapers and journals in the West, but these have never been very frequent and, after 9/11, have

* The Tiananmen massacre has conveniently become a distant memory, though it happened only yesterday and we saw it unfold live on our TV sets. And, let us not forget that the perpetrating regime is still in power. Academics and journalists write about it with a "detachment" and a "historical distance" that they could not of the Holocaust or the Nanjing massacre, both of which took place more than a half-century ago, and where the responsible regimes have been overthrown and discredited, and most individual perpetrators judged and punished. Nicholas Kristof in an Op-Ed in *The New York Times* (Aug. 29, 2003) maintains that though he was outraged as anyone by the Tiananmen massacre, in balance "authoritarian orderliness" was preferable to "democratic chaos." Kristof's is the sort of glib, impatient intellectualism that helped undermine the democracies in pre-World War II Europe and contributed to the rise of Mussolini and Hitler.

become even less so. They are also often buried somewhere on the inside pages and by and large receive little or no op-ed or editorial attention. Furthermore, there is almost no effort at a follow-up of any kind. Today we may read a report on the commitment and "treatment" of labor organizers in a police-run mental asylum and become duly shocked and horrified, but by the time we get the next report from China some months later of large-scale imprisonment and executions of Falun Gong adherents we have half-forgotten the earlier story, and generally fail to make the connection between the two — or with other accounts we may have read earlier.

Let us say that you were at the edge of a great forest, but somehow a bizarre neurological condition (*à la* Oliver Sacks) limited you to seeing only one tree at a time, and that too only in between disorienting intervals of time. Naturally your appreciation of the grandeur of nature would not be as wholehearted as someone who could see the forest as well as the trees, all at the same time.

So this anthology of China's human rights violations and other crimes, presented in memory-convenient précis, is essentially intended as a perspective-restoring tonic. Presented like this in a handy catalogue form it is hoped that the reader will come to grasp the totality of the Beijing regime's crimes, which in their sheer scale, variety, sophistication, pitilessness, self-serving expediency, profitability and the matter-of-fact calculated deliberation that has engendered them, make the thuggish brutality and murderousness of other authoritarian regimes around the world (yes, even Saddam Hussein's) seem crude and self-defeating in comparison.

Most of the facts presented in the book have been taken from the reports and publications of the Laogai Foundation, Human Rights Watch, Amnesty International, National Labor Committee, A.F.L.-C.I.O., Freedom House, China Rights

Forum, Human Rights in China, Cardinal Kung Foundation, Carnegie Endowment for International Peace, Tibet Information Network, Tibetan Centre for Human Rights and Democracy, Independent Tibet Network, Uyghur Information Agency, Geneva Initiative on Psychiatry and other human rights, religious, labor, intelligence, government, educational, advocacy and research organizations, as well as individual experts and scholars. A great deal of information has also been culled from the pages of *The New York Times, Washington Post, South China Morning Post, Business Week, The Economist, International Herald Tribune, Boston Globe, Taipei Times, Far Eastern Economic Review, People's Daily* and other newspapers, journals and news agencies worldwide. No original research has been attempted.

In the previous pamphlet, few citations were provided in the interest of reader convenience, but a China supporter in this country began to circulate e-mails to various Tibet-related organizations insisting that the pamphlet was spreading vicious lies about China. So, copious source citations have been provided this time around. Readers might be irritated by all those pesky little numbers perched on the edge of words and sentences like feeding mosquitoes, but it is requested that they put up with them in the greater interest of intellectual irrefutability and the shutting up of China's propagandists in the West.

And, there are a lot of them out there. Leading the pack is, without question, Rupert Murdoch, the world's most powerful media baron, whose 130 English-language newspapers (which include the *Times* of London and the *New York Post*), the largest group of television stations in the US (including Fox News Channel and Fox Broadcasting), and ownership or major interest in satellite services reaching Asia, Europe, and North and South America make up a sizable chunk of the world media. According to the comedian and writer Al Franken, Murdoch long ago recognized "which side his rice is buttered on"[1] and is essentially a retailer of Chinese propaganda, even entering into a multimillion dollar joint venture with the Party propaganda organ, the *People's Daily*, to help bring official Chinese government propaganda into the Digital Age. "The truth is — and we Americans don't like to admit it — that authoritarian societies can work,"[2] Murdoch admonishes critics. Even *Fortune* magazine has accused Murdoch of "pandering to China's repressive regime to get his programming into that vast market."[3]

In relatively more "liberal" quarters, we have Fareed Zakaria, editor of *Newsweek International*, who has been charged with asserting that "the Chinese people are dangerous, and best kept on a short leash by their government."[4] The Communist Party of China, Zakaria maintains, is a "liberal autocracy," an institution which he considers preferable to most of the imperfect democracies (India being his chief example) in the world today.

When questioned about the condemnatory tone of *The Economist's* reports on Italian Prime Minister, Silvio Berlusconi, the editor Bill Emmot replied that Berlusconi had betrayed the two things the magazine stood for: capitalism and democracy.[5] On reflection, this charge could perhaps be leveled at the very media watchdogs of the two institutions in question. Though perhaps not as fawningly accommodating of China as Murdoch's minions, most representatives of the international news-media (including *The Economist*) did, with varying degrees of emphasis and regularity, promote the comforting (and erroneous) beliefs that free trade would inevitably bring about democracy in China, and that justice, human rights, and even democracy were perhaps not so important in the context of Chinese cultural values, or in the greater interest of continued trade.

And, let us not forget China's lobbyists (or consultants as they prefer to be called) in Washington, D.C.: former Assistant Secretary of State Richard Holbrooke, former Secretary of State Alexander Haig, former Secretary of Defense James Schlessinger, former Treasury Secretary Michael Blumenthal, former Agriculture Secretary Bob Bergland, and even former President George H.W. Bush himself, his National Security Advisor Brent Scowcroft and his Trade Representative Carla Hills, among many other distinguished Americans whose services to Beijing have been rewarded with *guanxi* access to the China market for their corporate clients. "But when it came to China lobbying, no one held a candle to Henry Kissinger…," the economist Joe Studwell maintains. He further informs us that in one deal alone for a US oil company in China the former secretary of state's consultancy firm, Kissinger Associates, stood to reap $40 million.[6]

Among others in the China lobby line-up, we should perhaps mention California senator, Dianne Feinstein, Congress' leading proponent of a policy of conciliation with China and her entrepreneur husband Richard Blum (who has extensive business interests in Shanghai) since both are regarded as friendly with the Dalai Lama and sympathetic to Tibetans. "Senator Feinstein has also been known to plead for an understanding of the Tiananmen massacre in which many hundreds (possibly thousands*) of protesters were killed, by comparing it to the American shooting at Kent State University, in which four students died."[7]

Unlike other repressive regimes in the world today as that in Zimbabwe, Burma, North Korea and lately in Iraq, China has tremendous influence internationally not only in media, business and political circles as mentioned, but in academic and

---

* If we include those killed or executed in other Chinese cities and provinces in the wake of the Tiananmen crackdown, the numbers could be in the tens of thousands.

intellectual ones as well. In fact, China's influence in this regard is so pervasive and so subtly intimidating that a leading American sinologist, Perry Link, of Princeton University has dubbed it: "The Anaconda in the Chandelier."[8] In an article by that title, Professor Link makes it clear how scholars, journalists, human rights lawyers, even "whistle-blowers" in the West find it daunting, sometimes impossible to write or speak in explicit contradiction of what the Beijing government has pronounced to be a "fundamental principle."

However one looks at it there are too many fears, conveniences, delusions and self-interests that affect our memory and perception of China's crimes against humanity. The hope is that this small *aide memoire* will help you to purge them from your system and further persuade you to undertake a personal boycott of "Made in China" products.

Apologies are extended to all non-U.S. readers for the American orientation of much of the viewpoints and conclusions in the book. It was done for a reason. America is the largest importer of "Made in China" products. Therefore Americans, in particular, must be made aware of their immoral and economically unhealthy addiction.

This book lays no claim to being an objective academic treatise. It is an advocacy piece, scrupulous regarding facts, but not too concerned about giving equal time or space to China's point of view, which, in any case, has become so unrelentingly pervasive as to be quite overwhelming. Regarding the question of "objectivity" itself, especially as it surfaces in most (especially academic) discussions on China, the book defers to the greater wisdom of Lu Xun, China's premier modern writer and supreme debunker of propagandists and poseurs. He said, "Whoever thinks he is objective must already be half drunk."

Introduction

(2001 edition)

This appeal to all freedom-loving people not to buy products manufactured in the People's Republic of China has not been made lightly. It would certainly be preferable if there were a more amicable way to dissuade China from its growing human rights abuses, its brutal military occupation of Tibet and its aggressive military expansionism. But since the USA's de-linking of trade and human rights and the granting of permanent "Normal Trade Relations" status (or "Most Favored Nation" status, as it was known earlier) to China, the few modest leverages there were to influence China's actions have been effectively relinquished. Furthermore, most industrial nations in the world have also made similar adjustments to their national consciences and policies as the USA has done — some having done so much earlier and more enthusiastically.

The United Nations has been completely ineffectual in restraining China and, in fact, generally behaves as if its sole duty towards China was not to give it any cause for offense. For instance, the Dalai Lama, a Nobel Peace Prize winner and the single most important world Buddhist leader, was refused participation in the 2002 UN-backed Millennium Peace Summit attended by more than 1,000 religious leaders from all over the world — merely because China demanded it.[9]

The prevalent argument that market forces and international trade would transform China into a free-market democracy has by now been completely discredited. In fact, the opposite seems to have happened. China's human rights record has worsened with each passing year of expanding international trade and investment in China. In December 1998, President Jiang Zemin made a clear categorical declaration to the entire nation that China would *never* tread the path of democracy.* To drive home the point, as it were, he repeated it a couple of days later, vowing, in addition, that China would crush any challenge to Communist Party monopoly on power. Immediately afterwards there was a nationwide crackdown on the publishing and entertainment industry and harsh punishment was meted out to those "inciting to subvert state power."** This flurry of hard-line activity came almost immediately after China signed the Covenant on Civil and Political Rights in October 1998. The last two years have also seen unprecedented and brutal crackdowns on religious groups like the Falun Gong and perhaps more significantly, on increasingly defiant industrial workers and rebellious peasants.

On Tuesday, February, 26, 2001, the State Department in its annual report on Human Rights confirmed that despite years of deepening American economic engagement with China, the human rights situation there had worsened significantly, with "intensified crackdowns" on religious organizations, political dissenters and "any person or group perceived to threaten the

---

* When speaking to the Western media, Jiang routinely mentions his admiration for Abraham Lincoln, recites the Gettysburg Address and unfailingly points out that he was "elected" as president of China.

On September 14, 2004, in an important speech to the nation, president Hu Jintao, also categorically rejected democracy for China (*BBC News* "Hu rejects China political reform" 2004/09/15 09:11:55 GMT)

** Political prisoners were formerly charged with the catchall phrase "crimes of counterrevolution," which, since 1997, has been replaced in a new legal code by "subversion of state power."

government." And, the situation in Tibet had worsened. Such increasingly negative accounts of China's human rights record have become a regular feature for the last few years of the annual State Department report.

A NON-VIOLENT BUT DIRECT RESPONSE

With governments and big business in the free world having seemingly given up the use of economic leverage to restrain China, one nonviolent way remaining for concerned citizens to exert some positive influence on China is through the power of the individual consumer. The campaign we are asking you to join aims at making consumers aware of the moral and political costs of buying products made in China, and securing their participation in an effective boycott of all such goods. It will also help to pressure businesses and industries to rethink their economic ties with China. Mobilization of this power will not only make an impact on its own terms but, in due course, influence governments and politicians to implement policies that could genuinely help to bring about democracy and freedom to the Chinese people, and restore Tibet's independence.

Economic boycotts have, on the whole, an impressive success record. Gandhi's *Swadeshi* campaign to boycott English textiles was one of the first effective demonstrations of the untenability of British rule in India. Gandhi's campaign caused much economic suffering in Britain. A large number of mills in Lancashire had to close down and many thousands were rendered jobless. But the moral righteousness of Gandhi's action was so evident that when he visited Britain in 1931 he was given a rousing welcome in Lancashire by unemployed mill workers.

The power of economic action was most clearly demonstrated in South Africa in the struggle against apartheid. The boycott and international sanctions hurt the black community the most, since it was the poorest and had the least economic cushion against outright penury and hunger. Nevertheless, the resolve of the

South African blacks and their leaders never wavered. In fact, even after Nelson Mandela was released and a number of important reforms put into place by President de Klerk, the African National Congress (ANC) called for the continuation of international sanctions until apartheid was completely dismantled and a transitional government was in place.

A clear example of international economic boycotts or sanctions genuinely benefiting a suppressed labor movement is the example of Poland, when the USA led the way in imposing economic penalties on that nation after the Communist government banned the Solidarity movement in 1981 and arrested about 30,000 Solidarity members. The liberalization in Poland that brought about an end to the Communist regime was prompted in significant part by Poland's desire to get rid of the sanctions.

Pro-democracy forces in Burma have been calling on all countries of the world for the imposition of an overall "South African-style economic sanction against the ruling military government in Burma." A worldwide campaign for a consumer boycott and shareholder pressure forced companies like ARCO, Eddie Bauer, Liz Claiborne, Macy's, Reebok and Petro Canada to withdraw from Burma. In January 2001, the Burmese military junta finally agreed to enter into negotiations with Aung San Suu Kyi, the opposition leader.*

The increasing reports of strikes in China's industries and demonstrations and riots by the peasantry — in spite of large-scale and savage reprisals by the state — clearly disproves the

---

* There was a major setback to this progress in May 2003, when pro-government protesters violently attacked Aung San Suu Kyi and her followers. The government claims it has detained Suu Kyi for her own safety. However, there is real concern for her welfare. The possibility of future negotiations seems, at the moment, not too hopeful. The near abandonment of human rights concerns in China by Western nations most probably encouraged the Burmese military government to harden its line against the opposition party.

oft-repeated (and somewhat racist) contention of China's apologists in the West that the Chinese people are satisfied living in a repressive state and only interested in their immediate economic wellbeing. If desperate workers are going on strike, without the benefit of unions and strike funds, and when striking is illegal and punishable to the extreme limit of the law, then it is evident that workers in China (and by extension, the peasantry) will approve and endorse any action from the free world (like an international boycott of Chinese goods) that, though possibly causing temporary hardships, is clearly aimed in the long run at helping Chinese farmers and workers to secure the rights enjoyed by people in the free world.

Even more so in Tibet. The question often asked whether the ordinary Tibetan wouldn't prefer economic gain to political independence, or even personal freedom, is not only mistaken but grossly insulting as well. We are not in a position to conduct a poll in that unhappy country, but so far in every public protest and demonstration in Tibet, in every protest song, dissident writing and clandestine poster, the single outstanding demand has been for Tibetan independence. The only reference to economics ever to appear did so in a dissident document which was circulating in Tibet in the late eighties:

> *If (under China) Tibet were built up, the livelihood of the Tibetan people improved, and their lives so surpassed in happiness that it would embarrass the gods of the Thirty-Three Realms; if we were really and truly given this, even then we Tibetans wouldn't want it. We absolutely wouldn't want it.*[10]

Three Direct Reasons Not To Buy "Made In China" Products

Even a partial review of China's myriad crimes against humanity should be sufficient reason for any morally conscious person not to buy products "Made in China." But in this long unhappy list, three offenses take on special significance as they are directly and inescapably tied to the manufacture of the products themselves:

1. products made in forced labor *(laogai)* camps and prisons
2. products manufactured in factories and sweat-shops run by the Chinese military
3. products manufactured by a disenfranchised labor force

Products Manufactured in Prisons and Forced Labor *(Laogai)* Camps

The fact that a significant part of China's export of manufactured goods originates from prisons and forced labor (or "Reform Through Labor" *Laogai*) camps is well known. Less well know is the exact extent, due to the near impossibility of obtaining statistics on these camps and their productivity. But thanks to the dedicated and courageous effort of Harry Wu, formerly a *laogai* prisoner for 19 years, we now know that the scale of labor camp manufacturing is not only huge but plays a significant role in China's economy.

The Laogai Research Foundation, established by Harry Wu in 1993, cites that in several thousand forced labor camps an estimated 16-20 million Chinese, perhaps ten percent of them political offenders, labor on prison farms, factories and workshops in a harsh atmosphere permeated by sadism, torture and malnutrition. In his first book, *Laogai: The Chinese Gulag*, Harry Wu maintains that "armies of low-paid, forced, highly efficient working prisoners play a very important role in the Communist government's 'socialist construction' ... Never before has there been a nation with a prison system so extensive that it pervades all aspects of national production, has such careful planning and organization, and composes such an integral part of a people's economic and productive system."[11]

Detailed information on the Laogai or "the bamboo gulag," as it has sometimes been called, can be obtained through the Laogai Research Foundation's reports and website www.laogai.org. The Foundation also issues a very useful *Laogai Handbook*, which is updated every few years.

It has been argued by China's apologists that prisons in the free world also make their inmates work, often in manufacturing goods that are sold on the free market. The difference is, of course, that first and foremost, people in the free world are not incarcerated for merely expressing their political opinions or practicing their religion in a peaceful and law-abiding manner. Secondly, prisons in the free world are unable, because of laws or public opinion, to exploit their prisoners' work to the necessary inhuman degree where it becomes profitable. Prisons in the West are, because of such limitations, and also because of the relatively high standard-of-living of prisoners, invariably, economic burdens on the state. In China, forced labor manufacturing is a thriving and profitable economic enterprise.

This efficiency is achieved through a harsh system of motivation and punishment. Prisoners' food rations are linked to their productivity. Even sickness is often taken as evidence of poor work attitude and such "work avoiders" may have their rations cut off or decreased. "No work, no food" and "Light work load, light rations" are the rationale of the system. Other measures to ensure productivity are revocation of letter writing privileges and visiting rights, solitary confinement, mass criticism, prolonged shackling of legs and hands, and often beatings and torture. Prisoners who are slack, or accidentally damage tools or machinery are often charged with "sabotage of state property" and face punishment or fresh charges.

Prisoners often work under horrendous conditions as revealed in video footages obtained by Harry Wu, which were shown in an

Emmy Award-winning TV report in 1991.[12] In one sequence, in an animal-skin processing plant, naked prisoners waist deep in vats of tannic acid are shown stirring animal hides in the chemical. Prisoners in forced labor camps are often not only undernourished but are often suffering from tuberculosis, hepatitis and other diseases. Inmates in Manchuria and Amdo (Qinghai) face sub-arctic conditions where unwary prisoners sometimes die of a frozen lung merely from breathing in the open.[13]

In a discussion on healthcare in prisons in the United States, Dr. Abraham Verghese, the distinguished physician and author noted how "prisoners are the only group in this country with a constitutional right to health care" ... and "...an inmate — even one facing a death sentence — might have a better chance at being referred to a transplant center." He concludes: "I cannot help thinking how fortunate we are that the debate in this country is about giving lifesaving organs to inmates, and not about the grisly practice of harvesting and selling organs from prisoners, as in China."[14]

Prison labor in China is not confined to manufacturing. In May 2001, local officials in Sichuan province admitted to *Reuters* that 39 miners trapped in a flooded coal shaft and feared dead were convicts who were working in a prison-run mine. The officials said they had little hope of finding the men alive. Chinese news reports on the accident have not mentioned that the victims were convicts, and the government denies the existence of forced labor.[15]

Among the welter of "Made in China" products flooding the free world it is a major problem to identify those products made in forced labor camps. One reason for this is that prisons and labor camps exporting manufactured goods have created separate and innocent-sounding corporate identities for themselves. This is probably why efforts to boycott only products made in prisons and forced labor camps have never had much success.

Three years ago, *The New York Times* reported that fully one third of paper clips used in the United States (and distributed by Staples) were manufactured in a prison in Nanjing by female inmates "who were not paid, and worked so many hours that their fingers were sometimes bloodied."[16] The manufacturing company, AIMCO, was owned by Peter Chen, a U.S. citizen.

A *Washington Post* report in 2001, mentioned a development in prison labor practices in China that has compounded the problem of identifying prison-manufactured products.[17] In recent years, increasing competition has made it difficult for prison factories to sell their own products on the open market. Rather than improving conditions for inmates, this has plunged them into greater misery, as Chinese prisons depend on their factories for funding. Prison authorities now contract with private companies to manufacture an assortment of such labor-intensive products as wigs and Christmas lights, and they are pressing prisoners to work longer hours.

"On occasion, inmates work throughout the night without sleep. It's very common to see inmates spitting blood and fainting from exhaustion in the workshops," wrote a prisoner in a smuggled letter, a copy of which was obtained by the New York-based group Human Rights in China. "After laboring for long hours under bright lights, some inmates sustained serious retinal injuries that have affected their vision. But the guards accuse them of faking it and force them to work until they go completely blind."[18]

One inmate who was released recently said prison guards have a personal interest in pushing inmates to work harder because budget shortfalls mean they do not get paid, sometimes for months at a time. "They set a quota for you, but if you meet the quota, then they raise it. You work harder to meet it, and then they raise it again," the former inmate said. "It's torture to meet these quotas, but it's torture if you don't meet them, too." Several former inmates said prisoners who fail to meet quotas or otherwise upset the authorities are handcuffed to basketball hoops in the prison yards, or to high railings in the workshops, their feet barely touching the ground. "We'd be working, and these people would be just hanging there next to us," said one inmate. "It was like a warning."[19]

Another inmate said guards force prisoners to prop up heavy doors for days at a time, or torture them by binding their hands tightly with ropes. Guards also put troublesome inmates in six-foot-square solitary confinement cells infested with mosquitoes in the summer.

On a wet depressing day in November 1992, Harry Wu visited the Nazi concentration camp at Dachau. He saw a dormitory where prisoners had slept, crowded together, five or six hundred people in one barrack, and the so-called bathroom where they were given five minutes a day to clean themselves and then get out. Just one sink and one tap. Hundreds of people waiting for dirty water. For a moment, he found himself thinking how conditions there were no worse than those in Chinese camps. Then he remembered that Dachau was a work camp for prisoners of the Nazis and he felt sickened. On his way out of the camp, he noticed the slogan on the iron grillwork on the front gate. *ARBEIT MACHT FREI.* He asked somebody to translate it and was told "Labor makes (you) free." He was stunned, and asked, "Are you sure?" and the person replied, "Yes."

"In China," Harry explained, "the slogan for our camps was 'Labor Makes A New Life.'"[20]

Products Manufactured by an Aggressive and Expansionist Military

Thousands of factories and sweatshops run directly by the Chinese military manufacture anything from toys to underwear to steel pipes, and export them to the free world to earn the foreign exchange needed for China's military modernization program. Researchers at the A.F.L.-C.I.O. have identified ten of what they call PLA (People's Liberation Army)-sponsored business groups in the United States, each of which typically has several subsidiary companies.[21] A number of these companies are distributors and import-export concerns. In 1996, two of these companies, Norinco (a Chinese ordinance company that supplies the PLA with most of its weapons and has ten subsidiary companies in the U.S.) and Poly Technologies (which is run by the PLA's General Staff Department), were linked by the FBI to a scheme to smuggle some thousand AK-47 assault rifles into the United States. Overall, the PLA has a global empire of more than 15,000 businesses.[22]

According to *The Cox Report of the House Select Committee on U.S. National Security and Military Commercial Concerns with the People's Republic of China*, released in 1999, Chinese military and intelligence, through such companies in the United States, have stolen American nuclear secrets to build long-range ballistic missiles capable of hitting the United States. Also stolen was a large variety of sophisticated technology including high performance computers, satellite technology, aircraft guidance technology for F-15, F-126 and F-117 stealth bombers and design information on America's most advanced thermonuclear weapons.[23] The report has not been without controversy. Though Cox and most Republicans claimed that the report was "understated," some Democrats and certain intelligence experts, though not questioning any of the information documented, have relegated them to being exaggerated "worst cases."[24]

The thesis of the 1998 *New York Times* bestseller, *Year of the Rat,*[25] is that China's clandestine acquisition of sophisticated American defense technology was facilitated by Bill Clinton's injudicious pursuit of campaign funds. The authors, Edward Timperlake and William Triplett, describe how the biggest contributor to the Clinton-Gore campaign in 1992 was a shady Indonesian businessman with connections to China's intelligence; why an American businessman working with China's missile program was one of the leading sources of funds for the Clinton-Gore reelection campaign; and how Johnny Chung, Charlie Trie, John Huang, and others suspected of ties to Chinese intelligence or Chinese organized crime were granted extraordinary access to the White House. The book raises many interesting questions though it does not satisfactorily answer all of them. But Timperlake and Triplett's research is substantial and provocative enough to leave one feeling fairly certain that had Bill Clinton's Republican inquisitors been a little less obsessed with his sexual dalliances and more concerned with actual issues of national security, they might have served their country and themselves better.

In March 2003, public interest in the issue of China's pilfering of US defense technology was briefly revived as Richard Perle, who headed a Pentagon advisory committee, was forced to resign after the discovery that he had been improperly advising a major American satellite maker, Loral Space and Communications, as it faced government accusations that it had transferred rocket technology to China. Perle had also earlier been retained by Global Crossing, the communications giant, to overcome Defense Department opposition to Global's Chinese ties that were regarded as national security risks.[26] The Year of the Rat had obviously not ended.

No regime today poses a greater long-term and fundamental threat to world peace than the Communist leadership in Beijing. These days discussions on the subject of global security invariably converge around North Korea, Iran and (at least till a year ago) Iraq, but realistically speaking these countries, though certainly capable of great mischief-making or even starting a war or two, lack the size, population, military capability and economic power to sustain a major war, let alone the next world war. This is the capacity, however, that China is rapidly beginning to acquire, and evident in the double digit increases in its defense budget year after year.[27] This threat to world peace is far greater now than when China was at its most ideologically belligerent under Mao Zedong. Whatever the revolutionary rhetoric of Maoist China, it lacked the money and the technology to translate its intentions into effective action. But all that has changed, and this change has come about exclusively through China's newfound economic power based on it sales of manufactured products to the West.

It is often not apparent to most that China is undertaking an aggressive expansionist policy in Asia and the Pacific. Yet the danger of a Chinese invasion of Taiwan is ever present, and one that will certainly drag in American intervention — if America is not to forsake its preeminence in the Pacific.* Though the

---

* In a recent article in the *New York Review of Books*, Nicholas Kristof offers this suggestion to president Hu Jintao: the invasion of Taiwan might not be advisable since Taiwan would be sure to fight back. Instead, Kristof proposes that China "manufacture a crisis" about the Senkaku/ Diaoyu Islands which are a part of the Japanese Island chain (but which China disputes), as Kristof is sure that Japan, which "has been so wimpish" would not put up a fight. He supports his proposal with the observations that "after all Japan is a country that every Chinese loves to hate," and that America would not intervene (and risk nuclear war with China) even though obliged to defend Japanese territory under the US-Japan Security Agreement ("A Little Leap Forward," *New York Review of Books*, June 24, 2004).

Taiwan question appears only occasionally in the Western press, in China itself, officialdom and the media play up the issue on a clamorous and near frenzied basis whenever elections are announced in Taiwan or the Taiwanese leadership attempts to assert its independence. During such events, newspapers in China regularly feature letters and petitions by Chinese soldiers (often signed and even written in blood) calling for an invasion of Taiwan.[28]

Renewed fears of China's expansionism are rising in South East Asia. For instance, China has laid claims and even occupied parts of the strategic Spratley Island chain sitting astride vital shipping lanes to Japan, Taiwan and South Korea. The Philippines have the strongest claim to the islands by virtue of their proximity (about 200 miles from the Spratleys) while China, more than 800 miles north, has claimed the entire island chain, and built a base on the aptly named Mischief Reef.

The Chinese have already seized and occupied another chain of islands further north, the Paracels, from Vietnam, and have also occupied parts of Vietnam's northern border territory. Although today Vietnam's relations with its giant neighbor have improved, especially in terms of trade and tourism, the uncertainties of China's expansionist intentions compels Vietnam to maintain an army that is the fourth largest in the world. China's position regarding the claims and disputes on the South China Seas is a dogmatic and inflexible one. David Shambaugh, the director of the China Policy Program at George Washington University, notes that "PLA analysts tend not to write about Southeast Asia and sub-regional security issues because China considers its maritime claim to the South China Sea to be a 'domestic issue.'"[29] Ross Munro, former *Time* magazine bureau chief in Hong Kong, has stated that "even today China still seems to classify her 'neighbors' into one of two categories: tributary states that acknowledge her hegemony, or potential enemies."[30]

In February 2004, the *Washington Post* reported claims by Chinese academics that the long-dead kingdom and civilization of Goguryeo, which once extended over the northern part of the Korean peninsula and the borders of Manchuria, had been an ethnic kingdom of imperial China. These claims shocked scholars and politicians in both North and South Korea, and fueled fears in those countries of Chinese expansionist intentions. Scholars interviewed said that China could be laying the groundwork to dispute the border with North Korea (especially if the government in that nation collapsed) and, if they found it to be in their interest, to claim more territory. "This is not the first time the Chinese have tried to do this," said Yeo Ho-kyu, a historian at Seoul's Hankuk University of Foreign Studies. "They did the same thing before they claimed Tibet. Now, they are trying to use history as a weapon to wield influence in an area that is historically Korean."[31]

Countries like Laos, Cambodia and especially Burma have already been drawn into the Chinese sphere of influence. Burma's brutal military regime is a particularly close ally of China and has allowed the Chinese Navy free run of port facilities on its offshore islands and to build an electronic tracking and surveillance station on the Coco Islands in the Indian Ocean. The Chinese are also modernizing Burmese naval facilities in Hangyi islands and Sitwe, close to Calcutta, to provide Chinese warships direct access to the Indian Ocean.[32]

This development has been a major shock to India's defense community. It certainly contributed to the statement issued by India's defense minister some years ago that China, not Pakistan, was the major threat to India's security. This comes over and above China's supply of arms to, and training of, insurgent movements in North Eastern India, and occasional military incursions across the border. On June 26, 2003, when Indian Prime Minister Atal Behari Vajpayee was winding up a "historic" six-day trip to China, a Chinese force crossed the Line of Actual Control (LAC) into the Upper Subansiri district of the northeastern Indian state of Arunachal Pradesh and captured some Indian border officials.[33] Nevertheless, Sino-Indian relations have improved in the last year with China making considerable inroads into the Indian market with its cheap exports, and, Indian firms hoping to obtain major contracts to supply China's computer technology needs. Still, with none of the outstanding differences between the two countries addressed in any significant way, Indian defense experts are advising caution.

David Shambaugh, a leading international authority on Chinese strategic and military affairs at George Washington University, is of the opinion that India's nuclear test of 1998 contributed substantially to a radical up-grading of China's threat perception of India.* In an analysis of numerous articles published in Chinese defense journals, he concludes: "The PLA has seemingly found a new adversary in India. The only question is how long it will be before Chinese analysts see the United States, Japan, Taiwan and India as acting in cahoots."[34]

---

* The irony is that India's nuclear weapons program resulted directly from two Chinese actions: the 1962 military attack on India and the 1964 explosion of China's first nuclear bomb. In 1955, India's top nuclear scientist, Homi Bhabha, was president of the landmark international Atoms for Peace Conference in Geneva. India's first nuclear plant (1957) at Trombay "seemed open and aboveboard. There was no secrecy about it." In fact, Indian leadership and the scientific community generally subscribed (somewhat naively in retrospect) to the Nehruvian vision of the upliftment of the third world through the peaceful harnessing of nuclear energy, while for two decades China's "...nuclear effort remained almost exclusively military." "The Chinese bomb hurt Bhabha's pride as much as his patriotism." Within weeks Bhabha was calling for a nuclear deterrent, and in a few months Indian prime-minister Lal Bahadur Shastri gave the go-ahead. But Bhabha's death and strong political and moral opposition to the program kept it on hold till 1974 when under Mrs. Indira Gandhi, India conducted its first test (Peter Pringle & James Spigelman, *The Nuclear Barons*, Holt, Rhinehart and Winston, New York, 1981, pgs. 377-378). After that single test India maintained a self-imposed moratorium till 1998.

A number of books on the subject of Communist China's military expansionism have seen publication since the late nineties. Two stand out for their impressive research and balanced perspective. *The Coming Conflict with China* by Richard Bernstein and Ross H. Munro, two *Time* magazine China correspondents and bureau chiefs in Asia, examines in extensive detail China's rapid increase in military strength; its continuing portrayal of America as it foremost enemy; its challenging positions on Taiwan and South China Sea; its sale of weapons to U.S. adversaries; its concerted efforts to hijack technology; and its rigorous attempts — often through American corporations profiting in China — to influence U.S. policy.

Hegemon: China's Plan to Dominate Asia and the World is a more historically-based work. The author, Steven W. Mosher, is one of America's leading scholars on China, and one who has, somewhat unusually, been outspoken on human rights issues, especially on that of forced abortions and forced sterilizations. It should be mentioned, however, that Steven Mosher is a controversial figure, whose work has been criticized by other, generally pro-Beijing or left-inclined, China experts.

Mosher demonstrates how the concept of the "Hegemon," a political order based on naked power, was developed by Chinese strategists 2,800 years ago, and how it evolved into a extremely sophisticated diplomatic and military strategy aimed at establishing "hegemon power" over all the states in the known world. Mosher argues that the Chinese past he has described is prologue to the present, and Western beliefs that China is headed for democratic change are based on wishful thinking. Mosher further demonstrates that American attempts over the past decade to fashion a policy of "strategic cooperation" with China came close to an appeasement that put not only Taiwan but all of Asia in jeopardy.

In conclusion, it might be said that China's xenophobia and aggressive nationalism has only increased since the two studies appeared. America's forays in Afghanistan and Iraq have strengthened calls in China for increased military build up. In an article entitled, "China Readies for Future U.S. Fight," *CNN's* senior China analyst, Willy Wo-Lap Lam, writes that "the Iraqi war has convinced the Chinese Communist Party (CCP) leadership that some form of confrontation with the U.S. could come earlier than expected."[35] Lam also mentions that President Hu Jintao indicated that Beijing must pay more attention to global developments so that "China make good preparations before the rainstorm ... and be in a position to seize the initiative."

In another article, "Why War is Reviving the Spirit of Mao," Lam writes that the Iraq war is reviving the spirit of Maoism in China and has created a revived interest in Mao's hard line policy towards "American Imperialism." "According to intellectual circles in Beijing, a group of scholars from think tanks such as the Chinese Academy of Social Sciences (CASS) is planning to petition the Communist Party and government for a bigger boost in defense spending."[36]

Though 9/11 has somehow allowed America to relegate the Taiwan issue to the policy back-burner, it would be rash to assume that China has done the same. In fact, Beijing has managed to take advantage of America's preoccupation with "the axis of evil" to advance it plans regarding Taiwan. This was made clear in a Pentagon report to Congress on July 30, 2003, which stated that China had accelerated production of short-range ballistic missiles not only to hold Taiwan at peril but also "to complicate United States intervention in a Taiwan Strait conflict. China had also vastly managed to exceed the previous year's Pentagon's estimate of missile production for the Taiwan front." The report added that China had increased military spending to pay for accelerated missile production, a fleet of Chinese-made strike aircrafts and advanced Russian warships.* "China's strategy," the report said, "is to prevail so quickly in any Taiwan crisis that the United States could not intervene effectively."[37]

On November 19, 2003, for the first time in more than three years, China openly threatened to attack Taiwan if its (democratically-elected) leaders pursued efforts toward formal independence.[38] On December 2, China's military leadership declared that it would "reunify" Taiwan to the mainland even if that meant pushing China's economy into recession or destroying its plans to be host to the 2008 Olympics.[39]

* This almost certainly refers to the Sovremenny-class, nuclear-armed, guided missile destroyer, Russia's most advanced warship, primarily designed to kill American aircraft carriers and Aegis-class cruisers. The U.S. Navy has, to date, no effective defense against the Sovremenny's missile system.

Products Made by a Disenfranchised Labor Force

Admittedly, many of the "Made in China" products we see on the shelves of Wal-Mart or Toys'R'Us are not manufactured in forced labor camps or by the Chinese military. They are made by ordinary Chinese workers. So where's the harm in that, you may ask? The fundamental issue is that the labor in China is not free. Workers in China do not have the right to organize, to form unions and hence to bargain, negotiate and, of course, to strike. All these actions are absolutely illegal, punishable by lengthy terms in forced labor camps and even by death.

In theory, virtually all industrial workers in China belong to labor unions. In reality, these are government-controlled organizations, their leaders chosen by the Communist Party. The umbrella organization for all of China's token unions is the All-China Federation of Trade Unions (ACFTU) headquartered in Beijing. Instead of representing the rights and interests of the workers, these official unions under ACFTU "serve to control workers by playing the part of hired thugs and public security in workplaces," according to an article in *China Rights Forum.*[40]

In December 2003, *The New York Times* published a lengthy report on China's "Captive Unions," and how "...police crush efforts to set up independent unions as threats to the Communist Party," and that "... the sole legal state-run union is a charade, a feckless bureaucracy that has only the pretense of representing the proletariat."[41]

The Communist Party's biggest fear is the rise of an independent workers movement. The Democracy Movement of 1989 saw the formation of the Workers' Autonomous Federation in Beijing, which quickly spread across the country at a surprising rate. During the subsequent Tiananmen massacre, many of those killed were workers and labor activists, and in the ensuing mopping-up many more were arrested and many executed, some executions being broadcast on national television. But from then on, the idea of independent labor unions that would represent the interests of their members began to gain currency. Since 1989, in increasing numbers influential dissidents within China have raised the issue of labor rights. Unfortunately, these voices are still weak and the authorities have shown a remarkable ferocity in cracking down on even seminal labor groups.

Unsuccessful as they were, a few of the early efforts should be mentioned. In May 1992, sixteen organizers of the clandestine "Free Labor Union of China" were arrested in Beijing, two of the leaders being Wang Guoqi and Hu Shigen, the latter a professor at the Beijing Languages Institute.[42] In 1994, this group of people received prison sentences ranging from seven to twenty years. In 1994, an organization called the League for the Protection of the Rights of Working People appeared in Beijing.[43] The organization's founders were all arrested after they openly tried to register their group with the government. Many in that group are still in custody. In May 1994, three workers were arrested in Shenzhen after they applied to register a workers' night school and a newsletter called *Laboring People's Bulletin.*[44] Their whereabouts remain unknown to this day.

This situation is no better, probably even worse, in China's agricultural sector. According to Jasper Becker, former Beijing

Bureau Chief for the *South China Morning Post*, "the 600 million Chinese peasants who live in that vast monotonous archipelago of villages across the North China plain and the provinces of Shandong, Henan, Jiangsu, Anhui, Jiangzi, Sichuan and Hunan probably constitute the largest disenfranchised group in the world. Openly forbidden to organize themselves to defend their interests against either the central state or local despots … the state seems involved in a continual battle to crush them, and from time to time faint reports of this repression reach the outside world."

In 1998 and 1999, peasant riots occurred all over Hunan province. In Qiyang county in the southwest, police opened fire on 10,000 farmers who had gathered outside Party Headquarters. There were also riots in Qidong, Wefushi, Dazhongqiao, Luodi, Xingxi, Xupu and Yizhang as well as Ningxing. Bombs exploded in many places, including one that went off in a bus as it passed the provincial Party offices in Changsha. Other peasants blocked railway lines.[45]

Yet in spite of harsh government crackdowns and punishment of individual workers, demonstrations and strikes by workers in industry are definitely on the rise in China. A Hong Kong-based labor source reports that "in recent years, many foreign-invested, collective and private enterprises have been in arrears in the payment of wages, and have furthermore faced a mounting burden from paying retirement pensions. As a result, they have forced workers to work overtime without overtime pay and this has resulted in increasingly frequent strikes and demonstrations."[46] But these were eventually suppressed by coordinated action by the government and employers.

In certain plants owned by foreign companies, corporal punishment is common. Girls in these factories work twelve-hour shifts with only two days leave in a month, and sleep eight to ten crammed in a dormitory room, which is locked at night.

Talking is forbidden on the shop floor and to go to the toilet or drink a glass of water requires a permission card. Sexual harassment is common and punishment of uncooperative workers can involve beating, confinement or cancellation of wages. Arriving late can mean half-a-day's wages docked.

An outstanding and extensive study of such exploitation of Chinese labor by Professor Anita Chan, one the world's foremost experts on Chinese employment relations, was published in 2001.[47] The many case studies, with substantive analysis, cover abuses in a wide variety of settings: state enterprises, urban collectives, township and village enterprises, domestic private enterprises and foreign funded enterprises. The cases include urban workers, migrant workers from the countryside and workers who are sent to work outside of China. Besides the praises of eminent Sinologists, labor experts and economists, John Sweeney, President of A.F.L.-C.I.O., had this to say of Anita Chan's book: "What is so vividly portrayed in the true stories Dr. Chan has collected is deeply disturbing, for it paints a world of extreme exploitation and little hope. For all of the believers in unbridled, free-market economic reform as the only path for China's economic salvation, this book is a must read."

The single largest importer of Chinese-made products *in the world* is the American supermarket chain Wal-Mart*, buying $10-12 billion worth of merchandise every year from several thousand Chinese factories. Charlie Kernaghan of the National Labor Committee reports that Wal-Mart's harsh labor policies were "actually lowering standards in China, slashing wages and benefits, imposing long, mandatory-overtime shifts, while tolerating the arbitrary firing of workers who even dare to discuss factory conditions."[48]

* Walmart has opened thirty-one outlet stores in China and has refused to allow its workers there to join even the government-controlled trade unions under ACFTU, claiming that the central government had assured the company that it was not required to do so (Carl Goldstein, "Wal-Mart in China," *The Nation*, December 8, 2003).

After conducting on-site investigations and interviews with Chinese workers at Wal-Mart affiliated factories in China, the National Labor Committee issued the report *Wal-Mart Dungeon in China*, describing the abysmal treatment of workers at such manufacturing plants. One particular section of the report on a handbag factory describes such things as:

> 14-hour shifts, 7 days a week; 30 days a month average take-home pay of 3 cents an hour; $3.10 for a 98-hour workweek; one worker earning 36 cents for an entire month's work; 46 percent of the workers earning nothing at all and actually in debt to the company; housed 16 to a room and fed two dismal meals a day; physical and verbal abuse; workers held as indentured servants; identification documents confiscated and allowed to leave the factory just 1 1/2 hours a day; 800 workers fired for fighting for their basic rights.[49]

The National Labor Committee also interviewed workers in Guangdong Province making popular action figures, dolls, and other toys sold at Wal-Mart, and later issued a shocking 58-page report entitled, *Toys of Misery*. The most recent such report, *Toys of Misery 2004*, is a detailed expose of Foreway Industrial China Ltd., in Chang Ping township that manufactures dolls of major league players, produced under licensing agreements with the NFL, NBA, MLB, NCAA, Nascar and the Colleagiate Licensing Company. Other plastic toys, especially small toy cars, were also produced by Foreway for Wal-Mart, Disney and Hasbro. Among the many abuses listed in the report were 18 to 20 1/2 hour mandatory shifts, mandatory seven-day workweeks, net wages of $16.75 for 100 hours of work, wages regularly paid late, with those complaining sacked.[50]

According to Jasper Becker, China makes 70 per cent of the world's toys and its exports, now worth $7.5 billion annually, have doubled in eight years. In addition, China exports nearly $1 billion worth of plastic Christmas trees, ornaments and lights, tinsel, plastic angels and bells, Santa suits, framed pictures of Jesus and Bible scenes. Hong Kong and Taiwanese companies that make goods for the likes of Hasbro (whose brands include Action Man and Bob the Builder), Mattel (makers of Barbie) and Disney have shifted production to the Chinese mainland, lured by the plentiful supply of cheap, unregulated labor. Dr. Anita Chan said: "People who buy toys should care, [because] conditions in the toy sector are probably worse than other factories."[51]

A February 2004 *Washington Post* report charged that "Wal-Mart and China have forged themselves into the ultimate joint venture, their symbiosis influencing the terms of labor and consumption the world over ... The Communist Party government has become perhaps the world's greatest facilitator of capitalist production, beckoning multinational giants with tax-free zones and harsh punishment for anyone with designs on organizing a labor movement."[52]

Deprived of the right to unionize or even to raise issues of workplace hazards with management, labor in China has been the victim of horrendous industrial accidents. "Thousands of Chinese workers are killed or maimed in unsafe factories."[53] Victims of such industrial accidents receive little or no compensation. "According to the Chinese government's official statistics (which, critics say, are conservative estimates), 6,121 people died last year just in coal mines alone in China. With numbing regularity, year after year, Chinese miners are killed by floods, fires, gas, collapsing tunnels and carbon-monoxide poisoning. Most miners are migrants who hail from the country's poorer regions."[54]

The growth of the migrant labor problem appears to relate to China's yawning income disparities. As inland incomes stagnate, peasants are turning to migration to boost their incomes, or even survive. Those from the remotest areas, who have typically not migrated, are now on the move as well. They are often the most vulnerable, having little experience away from their villages. A recent *New York Times* report spoke of more than 100 million migrant workers nationwide.[55] Such migrant workers, who do not possess registration papers, are the principal labor force employed in the export sector industries. China's household registration, or *hukou*, system gives workers few rights or recourse to protection once they leave their designated place of residence. In a country where labor has no rights to begin with, unregistered migrant labor is the easiest of prey to greedy employers, brutal policemen and corrupt officials. It has also encouraged an attitude, already existing from the country's strong local sensibilities, of viewing migrants as second-class citizens and ignoring their plight.

In addition to exploitation by China's export-oriented industries, the proliferation of non-registered migrant labor has given rise in numerous parts of China to the revival of actual slavery. Operators typically lure unsuspecting peasants with promises of high pay, good food and housing. Once there, they confiscate their identity papers and lay down strict rules of movement. Through threats of violence or death, victims are forced to work. "Once people have lost their personal freedom and are being threatened with violence, their calculations change," says economist Hu Shudong of the China Economic Research Centre at Beijing University, who has been studying this phenomenon of resurgent slavery. "They are happy to get just one extra piece of bread or to avoid a beating."[56]

A report by China Labor Watch,[57] also published in *The New York Times* (February 9, 2001), details the case of a labor activist, Cao Maobing, who was the spokesman for several hundred angry workers at the Funing County Silk Mill in Jiangsu Province, which had laid off many employees but had failed to pay required stipends and pensions. The workers accused management of corruption and the government-run union of collusion, and declared their intentions of forming an independent labor union. Mr. Cao was then forcibly taken by police to No. 4 Psychiatric Hospital in Yancheng, where, diagnosed as suffering from "paranoid psychosis," he remains in strict custody and has been medicated and forced to undergo electroshock therapy.

On December 22, 2002, in Dafeng, in northern China, a combined force of police and paramilitary forces ended a weeklong strike by storming the Shuangfeng Textile Factory, dragging out and beating protesting workers. Many of the workers were arrested, while earlier individual workers targeted as possible labor leaders were taken from their homes and presumably incarcerated. This is one incident among many of the "high tide"[58] of labor unrest recently being reported from China.

In recognition of the gravity of the labor situation in China, *The New York Times*, beginning on April 7, 2003, published a series of articles examining the cruel exploitation of China's industrial workers. This series entitled, "The World's Sweatshop," is online at nytimes.com/world. One article in the series tells the story of two farm girls lured to work for a South Korean eyelash manufacturer in Anshan city in northeastern China, and ending up in a prison-like factory working for a monthly pay of $24, minus a $14 charge for room and board. The contract also demanded that workers pay the boss $58 if they left before the end of the yearlong contract, and $2,400 if they "stole intellectual property," by working for another eyelash maker. The girls, Ma Pinghui and Wei Qi, both 16, tried to escape by climbing down a high window but fell. Both suffered broken legs and vertebral injuries. The article observes that such abuse is common in China's export industries and that officialdom rarely ever intervenes on behalf of the abused. In point of fact, the two girls "were rebuffed when they asked Anshan government and police officials to investigate the case."[59]

On March 16, 2004, the A.F.L.-C.I.O. filed a 105-page complaint to press President Bush to punish China for violating workers' rights by suppressing strikes, banning independent trade unions and not enforcing minimum wage laws. The A.F.L.-C.I.O. argues that this illegal repression of workers' rights translates into a 43 percent cost advantage on average for China's exports. This is the first case ever filed under the Trade Act of 1974 that seeks penalties over violations of workers' rights. The A.F.L.-C.I.O. complaint sketches a nightmarish picture of factory workers in China: millions of peasants who migrated to urban factory jobs treated as bonded laborers, forced to live in prison-like dormitories, working 18 hours days for half the minimum wage, and labor leaders often arrested and tortured.

"American workers are suffering, they're losing their jobs, they're losing hope," said Barbara Shailor, the A.F.L.-C.I.O.'s director of international affairs. "At the same time, Chinese workers are suffering under repressive conditions and are denied their most fundamental rights."[60]

China is now resorting to anti-terror measures to clampdown on workers and dissidents expressing their grievances in the only ways left to them — violent action. In a report by Willy Wo-Lap Lam of *CNN*, the methods employed by many of these members of disadvantaged and marginalized sectors of society, such as the chronically unemployed, have included explosives, poison, arson, hijacking and assassination. "Now, quite a number of desperate citizens have taken to airing their grievances by letting off explosives in a crowded place in a big city. Beijing's nightmare is that the terminally frustrated and disaffected may band together and form guerrilla-style urban terrorist groups."[61]

The plight of China's rural work force is the subject of a recent (2004) publishing sensation in China. *Zhongguo Nongmin Diaocha (An Investigation of China's Peasantry)* by husband-and-wife authors, Chen Guidi and Wu Chuntao, vividly exposes the cruel exploitation and misery of China's 750 million peasants, and has shocked urban readers. The government ordered the publishers to cease printing at the peak of the book's popularity this spring, but millions of pirated copies have since flooded the market. The names of the authors have stopped appearing in the news media, and the authors claim to being harassed by security agents. Chen and Wu are now being sued for libel by a ranking official. "In a country that does not protect a right to criticize those holding power, it is a case they say they are sure to lose,"[62] says *New York Times* correspondent, Joseph Kahn.

Other Reasons Not To Buy "Made In China" Products

Repression of All Religions

The Communist Party of China has always regarded religion as a dangerous and unacceptable challenge to its exclusive right to the loyalty and even devotion of the Chinese people. Although the Chinese constitution guarantees freedom of religion, in actual practice every religious group has to undergo an onerous registration process and their activities are rigorously monitored. Printing and distribution of religious publications are strictly controlled by the government. Any group seen as attempting to move away from the strict and intrusive controls the Chinese government exercises is immediately charged with "criminal activities" or "illegal gatherings." This invariably results in police action, with routine physical abuse, torture and long-term imprisonment of religious leaders and practitioners. Official demolition of churches, monasteries and mosques are not uncommon.

Human Rights Watch/Asia has published a useful handbook on the subject, *China: State Control of Religion*, in addition to other reports on this issue.[63] The handbook is essential reading for a fundamental understanding of the means by which the Communist Party of China suppresses, controls and perverts religious beliefs. Information on the persecution of specific religions and sects is available through agencies related to these religious bodies, chief among them being Tibet Information

News Network (TIN), Cardinal Kung Foundation, Free Church for China, Falun Dafa Information Center, Tibetan Centre for Human Rights and Democracy (TCHRD), Uyhgur (Uighur) Information Center and others.

On February 11, 2002, Freedom House in Washington, D.C. released a report analyzing seven Chinese government documents.[64] These secret documents, issued between April 1999 and October 2001. detail the goals and actions of China's national, provincial and local security officials in repressing religion. They demonstrate that China's government, at the highest levels, aims to repress religious expression outside its control and is using more determined, systematic and harsher criminal penalties in this effort. Hu Jintao (now president of China), regarded by some China observers as a member of a younger, more liberal generation of communist party leaders, is quoted in the document as endorsing the drive against the Real God Church (Document 4).

"These documents provide irrefutable evidence that China remains determined to eradicate all religion it cannot control, using extreme tactics," said the Center for Religious Freedom (Freedom House) Director Nina Shea. "Normal religious activity is criminalized and, as the December death sentences brought against South China church Pastor Gong Shengliang and several of his co-workers attest, the directives outlined in these documents are being carried out with ruthless determination."

On August 8, 2003, the Commission on International Religious Freedom (a U.S. federal agency) called off its proposed visit to China after the Chinese authorities imposed "unacceptable last-minute conditions."[65] A visit to Hong Kong by the group was also blocked by China. Michael K. Young, the chairman of the commission said: "It further raises the concern that just years after the handover, Hong Kong's autonomy is already seriously in doubt." In light of the fact that China had previously permitted similar Congressional and State Department bodies on religious freedoms to visit China, these restrictions could reflect a hardening of Beijing's anti-religion policies and a new attitude of rejecting the concerns of the outside world on such matters.

POPULAR INDIGENOUS RELIGIONS

On February 8, 2001, *The New York Times* reported that seven more members of the outlawed Falun Gong spiritual group had died in custody, raising the known death toll to 112. Four reportedly died in forced labor camps, while two were apparently injured during force-feeding to break up a hunger-strike attempt. As of June 27, 2001, Falun Gong claimed that some 234 practitioners had died suspicious deaths in custody or immediately following release. To date, many thousands of members have been detained (for varying periods), while at least ten thousand are serving lengthy terms in forced labor camps. An unknown number have been committed to psychiatric detention centers.[66] Beatings and torture of those arrested are routine and have resulted in many deaths. The massive and brutal crackdown of the Falun Gong and the intensity of the campaign blitz (in nationwide public demonstrations and mass meetings) with even far-flung regions having to demonstrate their active antagonism to the sect, recall the Maoist campaigns of the 50s and 60s.

By September 2001, the Falun Gong movement in China, with the rare exception of a determined group or two, had been forced underground. In addition to the harsh and intensive crackdown, a sophisticated nationwide propaganda campaign successfully demonizing the spiritual group and its leader, Li Hongzhi, and extolling the benign treatment afforded Falun

Gong followers in "bright, cheerful" reeducation camps, ensured that the Chinese public would go along with the government's crackdown of this "evil cult" (as former President Jiang Zemin called it). Yet as Human Rights Watch put it: "The internal propaganda campaign not withstanding, Chinese officials continued to violate the right to freedom of association, assembly, expression, and belief; freedom from torture, ill-treatment and arbitrary detention; and the right to due process and a fair trial."[67]

While the Falun Gong is the most well-known indigenous religious group facing persecution in China, it is certainly not alone. In Sichuan province in the late 1980s, the One Unity Way (Yiguan Dao) spiritual movement was ruthlessly crushed by provincial security forces, with its leaders being executed and thousands of its members being sentenced to forced labor. In a recent (2004) book, *Falun Gong: The End of Days*, the author, Maria Hsia Chang, professor of political science at the University of Nevada, tells us that "185 different qigong groups were 'wiped out' in Shaanxi province alone in 2000. Like Falun Gong, most of them combined the practice of breathing exercises with neo-Buddhist and Daoist beliefs. Among them were China Cultivation (Zhong Gong), Nation Cultivation (Guo Gong), Compassion Cultivation (Cibei Gong), Fragrant (Xiang) Gong, Blue Law Society (Falan Hui), and the Goddess of Mercy Law Sect." Fragrant Gong reportedly had over 10 million members. Its leader Tian Ruishing, has been missing since April 2001. Another group, Zhong Gong, claiming a membership 38 million, briefly became the object of international media attention in the late 1990s when its founder Zhang Hongbao fled to Guam and applied for U.S. political asylum.

TIBETAN BUDDHISM

Tibetan Buddhists have for the last few years been subjected to an intensely harsh, well-planned and coordinated campaign to crush their religion and culture. This was locally termed the "second cultural revolution" because of its severity, and the Dalai Lama has denounced it as "cultural genocide."

Arrests, savage beatings, torture of monks and rape of nuns in custody, and occasional executions are routine. Moreover, there is strict official regulation of religious life, which includes daily political reeducation of monks and nuns (conducted by State Security or military units permanently stationed at the monasteries or nunneries), a complete ban on pictures of the Dalai Lama, a ban on maintenance of household shrines or religious objects for anyone in official employment, and a rigorous and intrusive supervision of the activities of all important lamas and monastic heads.

But the escapes in 2001 of two of Beijing's show-case religious leaders in Tibet, the young Karmapa lama and Agya Rinpoche, abbot of Kumbum monastery, to the free world forced a temporary lull in the campaign while a reassessment took place. The pause was a brief one. In the summer of 2001, Chinese officials commenced a crackdown on the Serthar Buddhist Institute in Eastern Tibet (Sichuan province) in the Larung Gar valley. Large contingents of troops, armed police and teams of Chinese officials sealed off the valley and began the demolition of more than a thousand dwellings and other structures. The Institute housed about six to seven thousand monks and nuns and about a thousand Chinese students and Chinese Buddhist scholars who were all expelled and forced to leave the area. The founder and senior teacher of this unique spiritual community, Khenpo Jigme Phuntsog, was taken away.[69] Readers should view the photographs of the Institute on the website of the Tibetan

Center for Human Rights and Democracy[70] to get an idea of the impressive scale of this deeply moving religious revival.

On Sunday, January 26, 2003, the Higher People's Court of Sichuan Province in Chengdu confirmed the death sentences given to the Tibetan Buddhist teacher Tenzin Deleg Rinpoche and his aide and relative Lobsang Thondup.[71] According to the Chinese official news agency Xinhua, the sentences were applied for "sabotage [of] the unity of the country and the unity of various ethnic groups" and "crimes of terror." Lobsang Thondup was executed shortly after. There is some indication that Tenzin Deleg Rinpoche may be executed sometime in December 2004 or January 2005.

Tenzin Deleg Rinpoche's real crime, however, appears to be the strong religious and moral influence he exerted over the people of Lithang in Eastern Tibet. Wang Lixiong, the Chinese author of a book on Tibet who has visited the region several times in recent years, said that in the mountain communities — dispirited by cycles of repression, poverty and alcoholism — Tenzin Deleg was revered for "showing a new path."

"What he did was to set a moral example, and that had a big effect on the people," Mr. Wang said. "But the government saw him as a threat."[72]

In February 2004, Human Rights Watch released a 105-page report, *Trials of a Tibetan Monk: The Case of Tenzin Delek*, that provides extensive documentation and information on this specific case and other crackdowns on religious leaders and movements in Eastern Tibet.

The child Panchen Lama, Tibet's second most important religious leader and one of the world's youngest political prisoners, arrested at the age of six, still remains in unknown confinement since 1995, the year of his secret abduction.

British writer Isabel Hilton provides a meticulously researched and moving account of this cruel and tragic event in her book, *The Search for the Panchen Lama.*

A first-hand report (September 2003) of religious repression in Tibet came from Philip P. Pan, correspondent for the *Washington Post,* who undertook an eight-day trip across Tibet and conducted numerous interviews. Some excerpts from his article:

"The government maintains tight control of Tibet's monasteries, restricting the number of monks and nuns who can worship. It has banned religious teachings considered politically sensitive and has suspended various tests that would allow monks to advance in their studies. It has also established Democratic Management Committees to run every monastery, though the monks who serve on these committees acknowledge that they are no longer elected by their peers."

"We don't regard it as democratic; the committee represents the government," said Nyima Tsering, deputy director at the Jokhang Temple, Lhasa's holiest shrine. He said the government appointed him and six other monks to the committee after evaluating their patriotism. Two government officials also sit on the committee and have the final say in any decisions.

"Every March, it (the Chinese administration) orders government work units to make sure employees do not celebrate the Dalai Lama's birthday, threatening officials with dismissal if police catch any of their subordinates doing so. The party has also banned all government employees from displaying photos of the Dalai Lama at home and has even tried to force them to take down Buddhist statues."

"At Tibet University in Lhasa, officials said students are prohibited from praying at temples or taking part in other religious activities, and face expulsion if they do. Even in high schools and middle schools, students are often told not to practice religion, residents said. The government is also trying to end the rural tradition of sending children to study in the monasteries."[73]

The International Campaign for Tibet in Washington DC, released in 2004 a report entitled, *A Season to Purge: Religious Repression in Tibet.* The report analyzes the structures and methods of Chinese government and Party controls over Tibet's monasteries and shows how the Chinese government is engaged in an extensive campaign to limit the spread and growth of Tibetan Buddhism.

The International Religious Freedom Report for 2004 was submitted to Congress in September this year by the Department of State. In its section on Tibet, it provides a detailed account of the numerous violations of religious freedoms in Tibet and of the various methods of repression used by the Chinese government. Also included were information on the arrests and imprisonment of nuns, monks and religious leaders as Tenzin Delek Rimpoche and Gendun Chokyi Nima, the Panchen Lama. The report maintains that "Overall, the level of repression in Tibetan areas remained high and the Government's record of respect for religious freedom remained poor during the period covered by this report."

CATHOLICS

Every day up to one hundred million Christians in China risk their lives by defying government orders banning free worship. Catholic organizations and congregations that recognize the spiritual authority of the Pope have been forced to go underground and Chinese bishops and priests and laymen have regularly been arrested, tortured and harassed. There have also been cases of outright murder of priests by security forces, as in the case of Father Yan Weiping of Hebei province who after his arrest in March 1996 was found beaten to death on a street in Beijing.

At least ten bishops and nineteen priests are presently confirmed as under incarceration,[74] while the fate of about forty more churchmen is simply unknown, with authorities refusing to confirm or deny whether they have been arrested or whether they are dead. Many more lay Catholics are suffering the same fate as their spiritual guides.

The frail 81-year-old Bishop Zeng Jingmu of Jiangxi province was rearrested on September 14, 2000, immediately following the completion of a three-year prison term. He had previously been imprisoned for 30 years from 1955 to 1995. On September 11, 2000, in Fujian province about 70 security police surrounded the house of an underground Catholic priest, the 82-year-old Father Ye Gong Feng, who was savagely tortured by security police until he fell into a coma.

In February 2003, Bishop Joseph Zen, the leader of the Roman Catholic Church in Hong Kong, said that mainland China had been stepping up its repression of the Catholic Church in China.[75] The bishop added that the Chinese authorities had closed down a Catholic seminary in China but faced a younger generation of Catholic priests who were less obedient than the older priests. On May 28, 2003, a China expert in Rome reported that Beijing had ordered stricter control over the lives of Chinese Catholics according to three government documents recently acquired.[76]

In a clear break with its previous conciliatory policy, the Vatican, on June 23, 2004, issued a strong protest to China over the recent arrests of three Roman Catholic Bishops – one of them 84 years old. The strongly worded statement demanded an explanation from China, and called the arrests "inconceivable in a country based on laws."[77] BBC religious affairs correspondent Jane Little said the Vatican response indicated that it had lost patience with China.

PROTESTANTS

All Protestant denominations are required like Catholics to observe the "three-self" policy, which demands that they abjure support from foreign missionary organizations, and that they give up theoretical, doctrinal, and liturgical differences to join a "post-denominational Christian church" loyal to the Communist Party of China. The "three-fix" policy requires that all congregations meet at a fixed location, that they have a fixed and professional religious leader, and that they confine their activities to a fixed geographical sphere. For non-mainstream Protestant groups, which rely on lay leaders and which recruit members through evangelical preaching, the regulation effectively checks growth and allows official monitoring of groups. Therefore, many churches have attempted to remain unregistered but when discovered have had their leaders and members arrested, beaten and tortured.

In the Zhoukou area of Henan such unregistered "house" churches have proliferated and with it an intensified crackdown on worshippers. In the first ten months of 1995, police in the area took more than 200 Protestants into custody. Their leaders were sentenced to three-year terms of imprisonment. The evangelical network in the Zhoukou area also has links outside their area. A November 19, 1994 police raid netted 152 church leaders, many from other localities and provinces.

On February 18, 1995, Li Dezian a preacher from Guangzhou had his church raided by Public Security officials. Five officers reportedly used a Bible to beat Li on his face and neck in an attempt to break his windpipe. They used steel rods to break his ribs and injure his back and legs, and jumped on and kicked his prone body until he vomited blood. All those present at the church — some one hundred — were dragged away.

Human Rights Watch/Asia has reported raids, fines and detentions from other provinces and cities such as Shenyang, Xi'an, Fuzhou, Guilin, Tianjin and several locales in Sichuan province, as well as in Shenzhen, the Special Economic Zone in Southern China.

In December 2001, two leaders of a Chinese Christian sect were sentenced to death, the first time such executions had been ordered under the country's 1999 anti-cult law.[78] Gong Shengliang, the founder of the unauthorized South China Church, and his niece Li Ying, were ordered to die in Hubei Province in central China for crimes including "hooliganism and rape," according to the Hong Kong-based Information Center for Human Rights and Democracy. Following a global outcry, the accused were re-sentenced on October 10, 2002, to life in prison. A *New York Times* report on the case drew this conclusion, "...diplomats said they thought that Chinese authorities were hoping to defuse international criticism, especially as Mr. Jiang prepares for the summit meeting with Mr. Bush in the United States later this month."[79]

More recently, Li Guangqiang, a Hong Kong citizen, was arrested for bringing annotated Bibles into China for use by a banned evangelical Christian group. He was arrested on the very serious charge of "using a cult to subvert the law," which can carry the death sentence. But in order to create "a positive atmosphere" for President Bush's visit to Beijing on February 21, 2002, Li was only sentenced to two years' imprisonment.[80] Two others, Wang Xuexiao and Liu Xishu, who were facing similar severe charges in Anhui Province, were given heavy sentences, according to Human Rights and Democracy, a Hong Kong-based group.

Many other indigenous Christian sects, as the Shouters,[81] the Disciples, Ling Ling Religion, Three Kinds of Servants Sect, the Holistic Church, the New Testament Church, and the Beiliwang sect have been outlawed and authorities have declared that they would be "hunted down and severely punished."

ISLAM IN CHINA

China has more than 17 million Muslims[82] but this figure is believed to understate the actual numbers by as much as 50 percent. The Hui are the largest officially recognized Muslim group at about 8.6 million and are ethnically and linguistically Chinese. Hui minority populations are found throughout China and they do not have a traditional territorial homeland.

The Uighurs are the most important Muslims of Turkic origin and are the dominant ethnic group in Xinjiang, numbering about 7.2 million out of a total population of some 15 million in the autonomous region. The Hui and the Turkic Muslims have different relationships with the Han Chinese and the two groups are not natural allies. The former are frequently referred to as "Chinese Muslims" and are culturally closer to the mainstream Chinese community. The Hui have no inherent connection with the Islamic groups of Turkic origin but have often served as a bridge between them and Beijing. Even so, the Hui have also suffered discrimination at the hands of the Chinese and have demonstrated their desire for greater cultural and religious freedom on numerous occasions.

In Xinjiang, because Islam is essentially indistinguishable from local cultural and national identity, Beijing perceives it to be a particular threat to its rule. As a result, mosques and religious schools in Xinjiang, which are regarded as hot-beds of anti-régime sentiment, have periodically been closed and religious activists arrested and harassed.

During the Cultural Revolution (1966-1976) in Xinjiang and throughout China, mosques were destroyed or closed, ancient religious sites desecrated and religious leaders imprisoned and executed. The situation improved in the eighties. According to Dr. Paul George, a Canadian researcher on international security and development, "Mosques were rebuilt or reopened and greater interaction between China's Muslims and the wider Islamic community was permitted. Chinese Muslim participation in the annual Haj pilgrimage to Mecca grew steadily from the mid-1980s, exposing many ordinary people to international Islamic thought and political developments. Similarly, foreign Muslims were allowed to visit Islamic sites in China, creating a greater awareness of the wider Muslim community."[83]

But by the early 1990s, mosque construction and renovation was severely curtailed, public broadcasting of sermons outside mosques was banned, religious education was proscribed, only religious material published by the state Religious Affairs Bureau was allowed, religious activists were purged from state positions and Haj pilgrimages were tightly controlled and limited to participants over 50 years old.[84]

Furthermore, the traditional Arabic script that had been used in the region for more than a thousand years is now being superseded by Chinese, and thousands of traditional historical books have been destroyed. The Uighur language itself has been banned in Xinjiang University according to the testimony of members of the Uyghur American Association to a U.S. Congressional Commission on China.[85]

The first serious outbreaks of violence directed at the Chinese authorities occurred in response to the imposition of these restrictive measures and reflected the local communities' anger and frustration at Beijing's about-turn on greater religious freedom.

"Whereas there has clearly been heightened awareness of their ethno-religious roots amongst the Muslims of Xinjiang in recent years, it is not apparent that this can be equated with the beginning of an Islamic fundamentalist movement," Dr. Paul George claims. "In fact, with some exceptions, Uighurs are not generally considered to be fundamentalists and the organized lethal combination of religion and violence seen in the Islamic world from Algeria to Afghanistan is so far missing in Xinjiang."[86]

Still, a small number of Xinjiang Muslims are known to have fought alongside the Mujahideen in Afghanistan and were also later connected to the Taliban. But Uighur leaders-in-exile maintain that the East Turkestan Islamic Movement, which the United States recently included in its list of Foreign Terrorist organizations, is an obscure group that most Uighurs know nothing about and that the political implication of this decision would be disastrous for the Uighur freedom movement worldwide, and to the ever-deteriorating human rights situation in East Turkestan. The editor of the Uyghur Information Agency in Washington, D.C., declared that America's action would "legitimize China's aggressive clampdown on any form of Uyghur dissent, no matter how nonviolent and peaceful it may be."[87]

On December 14, 2003, China issued its first formal list of terrorists, accusing four Muslim freedom fighting groups from East Turkestan and 11 individuals of committing violence and acts of terror, while calling on other nations to help in cracking down on them. Critics accuse China of restricting speech and rights of Uighurs. "We're really concerned about this," said Sarah Davis, a researcher with Human Rights Watch in New York. "Since Sept. 11, China has increasingly been equating peaceful movements for separatism with international terrorism."[88]

Forced Abortions and Forced Sterilizations

China, as a whole, commits about half a million third-trimester (seventh to ninth month) abortions annually. Most of these babies are fully alive when they are killed, and virtually all of these abortions are performed against the mother's will. Women are often imprisoned, brainwashed and refused food until they finally break down and agree to an abortion.[89]

The actual methods by which the doctors carry out the "procedures" are brutal. An injection of Rivalor, commonly known as the "poison shot" causes the baby to slowly die over the course of two to three days at which time it is delivered dead. Pure formaldehyde is also injected into the soft spot on the baby's head, or the skull is crushed by the doctor's forceps. Doctors in China are known to carry a few "chokers" in their pockets. These are similar to garbage-bag ties but longer. They are placed around the baby's neck and twisted, effectively strangling the child. Two other methods of aborting a child are by drowning the newborn in a bucket of water in plain view of the mother and also suffocation by towels forced into the baby's mouth as the doctor plugs the newborn's nose. The latter two methods are used especially to "teach a lesson in obedience" and also to act as a reminder that the People's Republic of China has strict family laws that must be complied with by its citizens.[90]

One of the first academic publications on forced abortions was Dr. J.S. Aird's, *Slaughter of the Innocents: Coercive Birth Control in China.* With lengthy appendices and 71 pages of footnotes the book is not exactly light reading. Using official Chinese documents (many translated here for the first time) as his primary source and through careful documentation, Dr. Aird makes an effective and disturbing case.[91] One of his conclusions is that between 1971 and 1985 alone there were some 100 million coercive birth-control "operations," including forced abortions and forced sterilizations.

For the general reader, Steven W. Mosher's, *A Mother's Ordeal: One Woman's Fight Against China's One-Child Policy*, comes highly recommended. *Kirkus Reviews* describes it as: "The compelling story of a young Chinese mother, giving a human face to the recent, chilling news accounts of how China has dramatically — and forcibly — decreased its birth rate. Mosher tells the story of Chi An in the first person, giving his dramatic narrative an even greater edge."

A dramatic revelation of China's inhuman birth-control policies came with the defection to the USA in May 1998 of Mrs. Gao Xiaoduan, who had served for fourteen years as the director of a so-called "Planned Birth Center" in a town in Fujian province. Mrs. Gao gave a detailed testimony to the House International Relations Human Rights Subcommittee[92] and also extensive interviews to American television and newspapers. Mrs. Gao confirmed previous reports that Chinese officials routinely subjected those who violated its one-child policy to forced sterilization and forced abortions — including women as much as nine months pregnant. Mrs. Gao revealed that the "Birth Center" maintained detailed files on the reproductive states of every woman under the age of 49. A network of paid informers slipped tips into a box about women in that area who had become pregnant without official authorization. She also added that in the first floor of the Center was a birth-control jail for women who tried to resist and also jail cells for family members or friends who might attempt to intervene.

Women who were reported with "illegal pregnancies" have been abducted from their homes by gangs of officials, who broke down their doors and dragged them away.[93]

Mrs. Gao managed to bring out videotapes and pictures, and with the help of Chinese dissident Harry Wu, smuggled out hundreds of pages of official documents, which experts in the field say are the most damning evidence yet of the kind of tactics used by China's planned birth program. It turned out that Mrs. Gao's defection came as she, herself, was in danger of being sterilized for violating China's one-child rule. She had secretly adopted an abandoned young boy, considered just as illegal as giving birth to a second child, and an informer had reported her to the Communist party.

Defenders of China's population control program often downplay state involvement by claiming violations as isolated incidents caused by overzealous local officials. Still, the extensiveness and uniformity of the violations all over China does point to a measure of official sanction for, if not direct central control of, the coercive aspect of China's population program. The following official statements and excerpts from official publications[94] appear to bear this out:

"So far the reduction in the PRC's rural fertility rate has been the result of external restraints: that is the mechanism involved has been a coercion-based reduction mechanism." (*China Population*, Beijing, 14th June 1993)

"It is necessary to forcibly sterilize those couples who have failed to be sterilized or use contraceptives." (*Politics and Law Tribune*, pp. 89-93, Beijing, April 1993)

"In order to reduce the population, use whatever means you must, but do it!" (Comments of Deng Xiaoping reported in *China Spring Digest*, New York, 1987)

The *Washington Post* report that 260,000 residents of Gansu province were sterilized because they were deemed to be "mentally retarded" by the authorities points to another disturbing aspect of China's population program — eugenics.[95] That population control was not the only goal of China's coercive program becomes fairly obvious in the following official statements:

"Mentally retarded people will give birth to idiot children." (Chinese Premier, Li Peng, *China News Service*, April 1990)

"The general rule is that idiots can't marry unless they are sterilized." (Chinese government official reported in *New York Times*, 15th August 1991)

"Raise the level of eugenics to a new height." (Song Ping, President, China Family Planning Association, *Xinhua* news-report, 20th November 1992)

"People of minority populations are more likely to be 'mentally retarded, short of stature, dwarfs or insane'." (Deng Bihai, *China Population News*, Beijing, 22nd December 1989)[96]

The last quote, suggestive of Nazi views on inferior and "sub-human" races, and theories of racial purity, reflects the racist views held by most Chinese of Tibetans, Mongols, Uighurs and other non-Chinese "minorities" in the PRC. It further provides substance to long-standing charges by the Tibetan government-in-exile and independent groups[97] of large-scale coercive birth control practices in Tibet. Such charges, it should be mentioned, have been dismissed by some pro-Chinese academics on Tibet as Melvyn Goldstein of Case Western Reserve University.[98]

Certain apologists for China maintain that, inhuman as it may seem, China is effectively doing what needs to be done to avert a population explosion, which could have serious global repercussions. Certainly, no sensible person will dispute that an effective birth-control program is necessary in China, but on the other hand there is every indication that such brutal and inhuman measures as are being currently practiced are disturbingly short-sighted, as female infanticide figures soar and earlier projections of drastic male-female demographic imbalances are beginning to be realized.

Valrae Hudson of Brigham Young University, in a study published in Harvard University's journal *International Security* (July 2002), noted that the 30 million unhappily unmarried men that China is likely to have by 2020 could become "kindling for forces of political revolution at home." There could also be an impact outside China, she says. The government may decide to use the surplus men as a weapon for military adventurism and "actively desire to see them give their lives in pursuit of national interest."[99]

Already the women shortage in parts of China has resulted in numerous cases of kidnapping and sale of girls and young women. A large black market in female babies was discovered in March 2003 in Guangxi province, when 28 baby girls (one dead, the rest in various stages of suffocation) were discovered packed away in the back of a long-haul bus "...being transported like farm animals, for sale."[100]

Research reveals that China's one-child policy has significantly failed because of widespread resistance by the peasantry with the collusion of local officials. In 1998, officials distributing emergency relief food in Paizhou county in Hubei province in the wake of summer floods discovered that the officially allotted quantity was not enough. The truth then emerged: there were 10 percent more people in the county than was recorded in the most recent census.[101] Critics of the coercive birth-control policies believe that widespread resistance and cover-ups has made the government miss its original target by 300 million.

It is also debatable whether China has actually done any better than countries that have not resorted to force and coercion. Fertility rates in India (also Brazil, Egypt and Mexico) have dropped sharply, especially in areas where good healthcare and education are available, particularly for women.[102] Moreover, India's average fertility rate is only marginally higher than that of rural China. In addition, India claims that its national family planning program has managed to prevent 230 million extra births and that its population will stabilize in 2040.

Extensive and Indiscriminate Use of the Death Penalty

China executes, on average, 40 people every week, according to an Amnesty International Report,[103] and throughout the 1990s condemned more of its citizens to death each year than the rest of the world put together.

From 1990 to 1999, Amnesty recorded 27,599 death sentences and 18,194 executions in China. "Many defendants most likely did not receive a fair trial and death penalties were carried out immediately after sentence was passed, thus denying the condemned the right to appeal," Amnesty said. Many defendants have been subject to torture to obtain a confession. Many may be illiterate and have little way of arguing their defense or understanding the process.

Amnesty also issues a separate "Death Penalty Log" providing a chronological listing of reports of death sentences and executions in China as monitored by the agency.[104] Amnesty recorded 2,088 death sentences and 1,263 confirmed executions in China in 1999 alone, collating the figures from public reports. These figures are, Amnesty admits, likely to be far below the actual number, as only a fraction are reported and the Chinese Government regards the total figure as a state secret.

Many have been executed for being declared guilty of what would be considered outside China as non-capital crimes:

corruption, rape, embezzlement, tax-fraud and even on occasions such minor charges as the theft of a bicycle. Such capricious sentencing usually occurs during nationwide "anti-crime" and "anti-corruption" campaigns when regions and provinces are required to meet certain quotas in arrests and executions. In 1996, the Chinese Government's "Strike Hard" campaign led to the execution of more than 4,000 people that year — an average of 11 *each day.* Subversion and ethnic "separatism" are also crimes that warranted the death penalty, especially in East Turkestan (Xinjiang) and Tibet.

In the "Strike Hard" campaign of 2001 at least 1,781 people were executed in four months, between April and July — more than the total number of known executions in the rest of the world combined over the past three years, Amnesty reported.[105] In this brief period, a total of 2,900 people were sentenced to death for crimes as diverse as bribery, pimping, fraud and "disrupting the stock market," as well as for violent crimes. An American tourist, Mike Melnyk, in Tibet during the "Strike Hard" campaign in May 2001, reported two children in school uniform, no older than sixteen, and one possibly even as young as twelve, being paraded through Shigatse town in an open military truck with other prisoners, prior to execution.[106]

The number of capital offenses on China's law books is believed to have grown from 28 in 1979 to 74 in 1995. Since then, non-violent and economic crimes such as speculation, bribery and the forging of value-added tax receipts have been added to the list so that the current figure is probably around 90.

"Most executions take place after mass sentencing rallies before huge crowds in public squares and sports stadiums like the Beijing Worker's Stadium, which may be the football venue of the Olympic Games in 2008. Rallies in Shaanxi province in April and May were reportedly attended by 1,800,000 spectators. Condemned prisoners are ritually humiliated by being paraded in public and insulted before being executed by firing squad or a bullet to the head."[107] The immediate family of the victims was, formerly, required to be present at the execution and to make a denunciation of the victim. This is no longer mandatory. However, the victim's family is still required to pay the cost of the bullet used in the execution.

The Chinese authorities are now switching from the traditional bullet in the back of the head to execution by lethal injection. *China Daily*, the country's main English-language newspaper, said the change "proves the country's respect for the dignity of all human beings, even those who committed serious offenses."[108] Other reports in Chinese papers emphasize the economy of the method. But, there is serious concern that the change may facilitate one of the most controversial aspects of Chinese capital punishment: organ harvesting from executed prisoners who make up the country's largest source of transplantable organs. The narcotic-poison mix used does not damage vital organs wanted for transplant. The condemned need only be given an injection of the anticoagulant Heparin beforehand, doctors say. With the proper preparation, even the heart could be transplanted if it were removed quickly. "I'm concerned with the shift to lethal injection because of the secrecy of the entire execution process in China," said Thomas McCune, a transplant doctor in Virginia.[109] He also noted that lethal injection puts the execution in a more controlled environment than is possible with executions by gunshot.

In an effort at cost-cutting and improving efficiency, Chinese provincial authorities are now introducing so-called mobile execution vans. The only previous record of such a facility ever being employed is in Nazi Germany where for a time mobile gas chambers were used in the death camps. Officials in Yunnan province explained that only four people are required to carry out executions in the mobile van. Eighteen converted 24-seat buses are being distributed to all intermediate courts and one high court in Yunnan province. The windowless execution chamber at the back contains a metal bed on which the prisoner is strapped down. Once the needle is attached by the doctor, an act which breaches international medical ethics, a police officer presses a button and an automatic syringe inserts the lethal drug into the prisoner's vein.

Zhao Shijie, president of the Yunnan Provincial High Court, was quoted praising the new system: "The use of lethal injection shows that China's death penalty system is becoming more civilized and humane." Members of China's legal community, however, fear that it will only lead to an increase in the use of the death penalty.[110] An additional reason for mobile executions could be to simplify transport of fresh cadavers to hospitals for organ harvesting. The whole process of loading up dead bodies from the execution grounds to ambulances could be dispensed with. In fact, one could now perform the execution on the way to the transplant hospital thereby saving valuable time.

During the SARS outbreak in China last year, the *China Daily* online (May 20, 2003) reproduced the official Chinese government proclamation that infringing the health regulations and spreading the virus would be punishable by 10 years to life imprisonment, or the *death penalty.*[111]

Commercial Harvesting of Transplant Organs of Executed Prisoners

In 1994, Human Rights Watch/Asia issued a 42-page report that charged China with using executed prisoners as its main source for organ transplants.[112] The report clearly demonstrated how any notion of "consent" to organ donation in China was absurd, given what it calls the "fundamentally coercive" situation in which persons condemned to undergo judicial execution are placed. The complete lack of judicial safeguards in China guaranteed that many people would be wrongfully executed and become unwitting organ donors. What the report underlined most disturbingly of all was that the practice of using prisoners' organs was widespread.

Citing government documents, doctors' statements and medical journal articles, the report revealed cases of kidneys having been removed from prisoners the night before their executions. It also cited cases where some inmates were still alive when their organs were removed, and that often executions appeared to be scheduled according to transplant needs. Some executions were known to have been deliberately botched to ensure that prisoners were not yet dead when their organs were removed. The use of condemned prisoners' organs involved members of the medical profession in the actual execution process, in violation of international standards of medical ethics. Patients requesting Chinese surgeons for transplants were often advised to wait until a major holiday, when authorities traditionally executed the most prisoners.

The report cited some disturbing case studies, providing the names and locations of hospitals and pointing out evidence of cases in Chinese medical publications as the *Journal of Chinese Organ Transplantation.* It even quoted Chinese government directives on the subject. For instance, one dated October 1984 states: "The use of corpses or organs of executed criminals must be kept secret... Guards must remain posted around the execution grounds while the operation for organ removal is going on."

This Human Rights Watch report caused a brief stir in the West but was soon forgotten. Still, stories of such atrocities somehow occasionally make it to the outside. One report was exceptional in the details and corroborative material provided. Zhao Wei and Wan Qichao were executed in 1999 in Henan province and their kidneys were harvested in spite of strident family objections.[113] A detailed eyewitness account by family friend Lu De'an of the executions and removal of organs, statements by the families of the two victims, photographs of the two men and photographic evidence of bags of "kidney preservative fluid," surgical gloves, etc., discarded at the removal site, provided powerful confirmation of an atrocity that was being duplicated thousands of times throughout China.

In 1999, Huang Peng, a Chinese prison official at the Shenyang No. 2 Prison, Liaoning province's largest penitentiary, fled to Russia. He gave a lengthy statement to Western journalists about his personal knowledge of the harvesting of transplant organs from executed prisoners. He also stated how military and paramilitary hospitals dominate the harvesting and transplanting, because they have close ties to the prosecutors and court officials who supervise executions. The hospitals obtain the organs almost free, usually by paying court officials a nominal sum, and charge thousands of dollars per transplant. *The New York Times* reported that "it is a boom industry. The number of transplant operations has soared in the last decade, and modern new transplant centers have opened around the country. One center established earlier this year in Hangzhou, south of Shanghai, specializes in multiple organ transplants for individual patients."[114]

In 1999, in New York City, the FBI in a sting operation broke up a bespoke service in the sale of organs of executed Chinese prisoners in which at least one senior Chinese official was involved.[115] Earlier in 1997, *ABC News* presented an exclusive report featuring a hidden-camera sting of Chinese doctor Dai Yong and his wife accepting, in a New York hotel room, a down payment for a $30,000 kidney from an executed Chinese prisoner.[116]

A news report in 2000, cited Dr. S.Y. Tan, one of Malaysia's leading kidney specialists, as claiming that more than 1,000 Malaysians have had kidney transplants in China from executed prisoners.[117] Transplant patients from Thailand, Taiwan and other countries are reported to be using such services in China, and there are indications that this trend is increasing. All reports point to the commercial nature of the transplant sales and affirm that organs are sold to the highest bidders, often foreigners.

In June 2001, a former Chinese Army doctor, Wang Guoqi, testified before a United States Congressional Committee.[118] Dr. Wang described how he had removed skin and corneas from the bodies of executed prisoners and how injections of the anticoagulant Heparin were given to the prisoners by hospital staff before the executions. After the prisoner was shot in the back of the head, transplant surgeons rushed to remove the liver, kidneys, cornea and other organs either in an ambulance at the execution site or at a crematory. Dr. Wang reported that he had witnessed doctors remove kidneys from a man who was still breathing. *The Times* article detailed mounting evidence that China was selling organs from executed prisoners, sometimes to Americans. "Transplant doctors in the United States report that an increasing number of patients are showing up for post-transplant care after travelling to China for organs, particularly kidneys, that they would have to wait up to years in the West."

A November 2001, report cites Dr. Thomas Diflo of New York who claimed that he had to provide after-transplant care to American patients who received organs in China from executed prisoners.[119] Dr. Stephen Tomlanovich, a kidney transplant specialist at the University of California, San Francisco, has also stated that several of his patients who traveled to Shanghai or Guangzhou had received kidneys that he suspected came from executed prisoners. The report mentions five hospitals in Shanghai that perform kidney transplants, and adds that they welcome foreign patients because they pay as much as ten times the price local patients pay for the same operation.

After the *ABC News* report in 1997 there has been an inexplicable silence on this issue on American TV. In an hour-long *A&E Network* documentary in 1999, "The Organ Trade: Life and Death for Sale,"[120] no reference was made to the commercial harvesting of transplant organs of executed prisoners in China. More recently, on a *CNN* program, "The Black Market in Organs" aired in September 2003,[121] the host, experts and guests on the show bemoaned the tragedy of the poor in India and the Philippines selling their kidneys to rich but ailing Americans, but did not make even a passing reference to the flourishing trade in organs of executed prisoners in China. In a similar program on *MSNBC* in January 2004, no mention was made of China.[122]

Routine Torture of Prisoners

The use of torture to extract confessions is routine in China's penal system. Furthermore, torture does not appear to result from random police brutality, miscarriage of justice, or anomalies in the application of the law but is inherent in the system. An Amnesty International report released in 1996 concluded: "We believe the law enforcement system and the justice system in China actually fosters torture."[123] China signed the United Nations Convention Against Torture and Other Cruel, Inhuman or Degrading Treatment or Punishment in 1988.

Methods of torture consist of solitary confinement in windowless cells too small to stand up in, kneeling on glass shards, electrocution with high-voltage currents, and some Cultural Revolution favorites like the "airplane" where one's arms are forced backwards and up till the shoulders pop from their sockets, and also being strung up by the wrist or thumbs for days. Older traditional methods like the bamboo splint under the fingernail, and extraction of fingernails, have made their reappearance according to the Amnesty report. Beatings with clubs and truncheons are normal.

In 2001, Amnesty issued a notably comprehensive report on torture in China.[124] This detailed study describes nine different categories of situations in which torture is used by Chinese police and officials. One such is in the enforcement of China's "one-child" policy. The introduction to the report describes the death under torture of Zhou Jianxiong, a 30-year-old agricultural worker from Chunhua township in Hunan province, on May 15, 1998. He was tortured by officials from the township birth control office to make him reveal the whereabouts of his wife, suspected of being pregnant without permission. Zhou was hung upside down, repeatedly whipped and beaten with wooden clubs, burned with cigarette butts, branded with soldering irons and had his genitals ripped off.

The 2001 report not only provides extensive case studies but also devotes two separate sections to torture of independence advocates and freedom fighters in East Turkestan (Xinjiang) and Tibet.

For women in particular, especially in the case of nuns in Tibet, torture routinely includes rape by security personnel. Furthermore, use of electric-batons on women's genitalia have been frequently reported from prisons in Tibet.[125] Tibetan children, some as young as nine, have been detained and tortured by Chinese security personnel, according to a study issued by the International Committee of Lawyers for Tibet (now Tibetan Justice Center) in 2001.[126] The report documents for the first time the routine practice of torturing adults and children arrested for "political" offenses. It also notes that children are detained in deplorable conditions, often without notice to their families, and held for months or even years without a trial or access to a lawyer.

An extensive report in *The New York Times* describes how China's periodic nationwide "Strike Hard" campaigns and execution quotas place huge pressure on local police to solve crimes quickly, which they often do by extorting confessions through torture. In Hunan Province, newspapers reported that the police solved 3,000 cases in two days in April 2001. Police in Sichuan province reported that they had solved 6,704 cases, including 691 murders, robberies and bombings, in six days that same month.[127]

Psychiatric Persecution of Political Prisoners

The first indication of this particular human rights violation in China came to light in 2001 in a report in *The Columbia Journal of Asian Law* authored by Robin Munro, a British human rights researcher.[128] The report, cited in a *New York Times* article of February 18, 2001, condemned China's practice of imprisoning dissidents in psychiatric hospitals. The *Times* article mentioned that "China has not been known for the systematic abuses of psychiatry that occurred in the Soviet Union, where hundreds of dissidents were spuriously diagnosed as schizophrenic and locked away." But, Mr. Munro reported that at least 3,000 people who were arrested for some kind of "political" crime were referred for psychiatric evaluation, with many of them deemed mentally ill and subsequently imprisoned.

Besides labor activists like Cao Maobing, mentioned earlier, and Wang Wanzing (diagnosed as "paranoid psychotic" for unfurling a pro-democracy banner in Tiananmen Square), the latest victims of this criminal abuse of psychiatry are members of the Falun Gong religious sect, whom the Chinese press have branded as mentally disturbed and requiring treatment. Such cases have even seen matter-of-fact discussion in *China's Journal of Clinical Psychological Medicine* in 2000. Hundreds of Falun Gong followers have been forcibly hospitalized and medicated according to reports from human rights monitors, and many locked away.

Mr. Munro's report has now grown into a 298-page book published by the Geneva Initiative on Psychiatry and Human Rights Watch.[129] The book is an "eloquent and convincing study," writes Jonathan Mirsky, who regards Munro as "the preeminent researcher in the field of Chinese human rights" and feels that *Dangerous Minds* (the title of the book) is his most impressive work to date."[130]

The book's evidence is drawn from hundreds of legal and psychiatric studies published officially in China since 1949. The report reconstructs the shadowy history of politically abusive psychiatry in China, with a focus of mental illness that was said to be caused by politically deviant thoughts; and it examines the reasons for the persistence of political psychiatry into the post-Mao reform era, when the official theory was that some dissidents commit their "crimes against the people" because of mental illness. The report also outlines the steps that the Chinese government should adopt in order to end these abuses, as well as measures that the international community — notably the World Psychiatric Association — should take.

A detailed analysis of the book is not possible here but two of Munro's findings are disturbing enough to require recounting.

In 1987, China's leaders, perceiving the emergence of an "ideological vacuum" within the populace, set up a network of police-run psychiatric custodial institutions known as the Ankang (the word literally means "Peace and Health"). These were essentially meant for the detention and treatment of dissidents and "political maniacs," but often included even "people who submitted petitions to the authorities." According to Chinese psychiatric documents cited by Munro, by 1992 the total number of Ankang custodial centers had risen to twenty, with several others under construction. According to one source, large Ankang centers can accommodate approximately one thousand inmates; the Tianjin facility, however, is believed to have around twice that capacity. The government's eventual goal is to establish one Ankang center for every city in China with a population of one million or above.

In 1986, Chinese hospitals began to perform psychosurgery, including prefrontal lobotomies. Munro cites a Western scholar, Veronica Pearson, who had personal knowledge of a large number of such operations carried out in Guangzhou, Beijing and Tianjin. Munro further states, "most worryingly, according to a reliable eyewitness report, the Ankang forensic-psychiatric facility in the city of Tianjin had by 1987 established a large and technically advanced unit for carrying out psychosurgical operations; the director of the institute at the time was a neurosurgeon, and dozens of lobotomies and similar brain operations were reportedly being performed on inmates there each year." Munro also provides official confirmation of the existence of the unit.[131]

On May 30, 2003, in an unusual public rebuke, the World Psychiatric Association called on China to fulfill its promise to let international experts examine charges that psychiatry has been misused in China as a political tool.[132] In August 2002, the world association, to which China's government-controlled psychiatric society belongs, voted to send an expert team to investigate the charges. Officials of the world association said the Chinese had initially agreed to cooperate and had provided written responses to some inquiries regarding Falun Gong members. But starting late last year, even written responses stopped coming, apparently on orders from the political authorities from the Ministry of Health in Beijing.

Military Occupation and Cultural Genocide in Tibet

Tibet, a peaceful independent country, was militarily invaded by China in 1950. After crushing all resistance, a systematic campaign was launched to destroy the Tibetan people and their way of life. This movement reached its crescendo during the Cultural Revolution, but continues to this day, in varying degrees of violence and severity. According to the latest estimates, over six thousand monasteries, temples and historical monuments have been destroyed, along with incalculably vast quantities of priceless artistic and religious objects — and countless books and manuscripts of Tibet's unique and ancient learning. Over a million Tibetans have been killed by execution, torture and starvation, while tens of thousands of others have been forced to slave in remote and desolate forced labor camps.

In spite of the Dalai Lama's many concessions and repeated efforts to negotiate on the question of Tibet, Chinese leaders have rejected all his overtures. Beijing's declared strategy now is to wait till the Dalai Lama dies, after which it is confident that the Tibetan issue could be terminated without international outcry. To ensure this, China has adopted a policy of deliberate subversion of Tibetan culture and identity, and the demoralization of Tibetans through unemployment, inferior educational opportunities, and unrelenting and ruthless suppression of the Tibetan people by the organs of state security.[133]

China's foremost strategy to ensure that Tibet remains permanently a part of China has been its policy of large-scale population transfer of Chinese to Tibet. Though earlier Chinese officials were adamant that nothing of the kind was happening, the recent success of this policy has emboldened Beijing to acknowledge the fact. A top Chinese planning official Jin Shixun, announced in Lhasa in 2002 that Tibetans would become a minority of the 200,000 people in their capital, Lhasa, in the next few years as ethnic Chinese migrants arrived in a drive to develop the economy.[134]

China's population transfer policy is being accelerated by the building of the world's highest railway line from Golmud to Lhasa. To be completed in 2007, this $2.4 billion project, Chinese officials claim, will bring Tibet "to the modern world." But a reporter for the *Boston Globe*, away from the ears of government officials escorting a group of foreign journalists at a press junket for the railway, heard from Tibetans that the initiative would only draw more Chinese settlers, "who have been migrating steadily to this area over the last decade, bringing with them karaoke bars, discos, and signs in Chinese script that most locals can't read."

"'The train is for them, so the Chinese can come here,' said a former herder from this northern grassland region through which two-thirds of the roughly 700-mile railway will pass. 'They are robbing our land of precious minerals and will use the train to take them away faster. They say they've brought us electricity, hospitals, roads, etc., but they are not for us; they are for the hundreds of thousands of Chinese who live here now.'"[135]

In the last few years, political repression has taken on new rigor with more arrests, torture, executions and vastly increased deployment of informers and security personnel throughout the country, especially in urban areas. Though such measures have been successful in suppressing large-scale demonstrations and the kind of violent "independence" riots that broke out all over Tibet, especially in Lhasa, the capital city, in the late 1980s and the beginning of the 1990s, they have been unable to contain public protests by individuals and small groups (especially young nuns).

More disturbing for Chinese State Security has been the rise of bombing incidents in Tibet. These started in the mid-eighties with random and often harmless explosions of crude pipe bombs, but which now seem to be gaining in technical sophistication and political determination, as evinced by the case of a suicide bomber who attempted to disrupt the National Minorities Games in Lhasa in 1999.[136]

Political repression, lack of freedom and even lack of educational and economic opportunities in Tibet has given rise to a steady stream of refugees fleeing across the high Himalayas to Nepal and India. On average about 3,000 refugees make this hazardous passage every year with many suffering snow-blindness, frostbite, loss of limbs and even death. A 2003 *New York Times* story stated that "last year, 1,268 Tibetans trekked over passes as high as 19,000 feet to reach Nepal, half the annual average from 1996 to 2000. Tibetan exile groups here attribute the drop to an increase in police on the Chinese side of the border."[137]

Most recently, China put pressure on Nepal to deport 18 Tibetan refugees back to Tibet.[138] There is genuine concern that the deported refugees would not only be given heavy prison sentences back in Tibet, but would also suffer beating and torture in jail. There is also grave concern that this deportation could set a precedent where Nepal would give in to further Chinese demands for the return of Tibetan refugees.

Draconian Repression in East Turkestan (Xinjiang)

In far western China, the Uighur (a Turkic people) have been waging a decades-long struggle to establish the Republic of East Turkestan. There has long been determined Uighur opposition to Chinese rule in East Turkestan. Effective control of the region by Beijing was not achieved until the creation of the People's Republic of China in 1949. Prior to this, from 1944 to 1949, a short-lived independent East Turkestan Republic, inspired by pan-Turkic nationalism was established in western Xinjiang.[139] (Xinjiang is the Chinese name for East Turkestan.)

In the past few years there have been more than 130 uprisings, according to Uighur sources. The Chinese have responded with a draconian campaign of terror to wipe out Uighur nationalism. Daily arrests and public executions are part of 'normal' life in the bazaars of the Silk Route today. Mass executions have been reported. According to Amnesty International, over 200 people were executed between 1997 and 1999.[140]

President Jiang Zemin visited Xinjiang in August 1998 and called for "a people's war" against the separatists, a call reiterated by Prime Minister Zhu Rongji a year later, when he called for an "iron fist" to crush the "splittists." Accordingly, repressive campaigns have been waged yearly, with renewed intensity, and gained a new momentum with the launch of the national "Strike Hard Campaign" in April 2001.[141] In its report, Human

Rights Watch mentioned its concern that China's support for America's war against terrorism could become a pretext for gaining international support — or at least silence — for its own crackdown on Uighurs in the Xinjiang Uighur Autonomous Region.

Besides the invariable human rights abuses, the "one-child policy," large-scale population transfer of Chinese people to East Turkestan, and Chinese racism, the Uighurs protest China's nuclear tests in the region, which they claim have been the cause of serious and unexplained health problems in Uighur society. China has conducted 46 nuclear tests so far, all of them in Xinjiang. One secret nuclear base located in the area of Malan is only six miles away from a residential area where ethnic Uighur and Mongols live. The director of the local hospital told journalists from Taiwan that many local residents suffered from hair loss and various skin diseases.[142] The number of patients found to have pathological changes in their blood was five or six times that of the other areas. The number of children and women with leukemia and throat cancer was also unusually high. And, the number of premature births and deformed babies had also increased dramatically since the construction of the nuclear base.

China's bacteriological weapons laboratories and testing sites are also located in Xinjiang. Ken Alibek, a former Soviet bacteriological weapons expert (now at George Mason University), has reported the discovery of two rare strains of Ebola and Marburg in Xinjiang, which doctors had never even seen in Africa. China began experimenting with bacteriological weapons as early as the 1980s. During the first years of the '80s, epidemics occurred continuously in southern Xinjiang and caused many deaths. Nobody knew the names of the epidemics, so they were identified as "No. 1 disease," "No. 2 disease" and so on, according to the year the disease struck. In the end, people simply dubbed the epidemics "unknown illnesses."[143]

World's Tightest Internet Censorship

On August 1, 2001, Human Rights Watch announced that tightening Chinese government controls on the Internet were having a chilling effect on academic freedom, commercial exchanges and ordinary communication. In a background report released that day, titled "Freedom of Expression and the Internet in China," Human Rights Watch reported that Chinese authorities had issued more than sixty sets of regulations to govern Internet content since the government began permitting commercial Internet accounts in 1995. The background report detailed many of those regulations, described recent Chinese efforts to police Internet cafes and summarized the cases of several people put on trial or sentenced to prison for downloading or posting politically sensitive material on the Web.[144]

An Amnesty International study reported that "Internet users (in China) were at risk of arbitrary detention, torture and even execution." Amnesty also provided a detailed list of China's Internet "lawbreakers" in this study.[145]

In a case last year that has "enraged human rights advocates" according to *The New York Times*, four friends, Xu Wei, Jin Haike, Yang Zilin and Zhang Honghai, who met on university campuses in Beijing to discuss politics and who posted occasional essays on the Internet were convicted of "subverting state power" and sentenced to long prison terms. The case has sent a chill through Chinese academic and intellectual circles, in part because the group's activities seemed to be innocuous and in part because the four men had been imprisoned for over two years without a verdict in their trial. The group had in no way posted any anti-government or dissident literature and their discussions and their Internet essays were about political theory. According to the wife of one of the group who visited them in prison "the four seemed to be in poor health, having lost weight."[146]

A couple of years earlier, in May 2001, Hu Dalin was arrested for posting articles on a Web site he had created for his father Lu Jiaping, 60, a retired army officer who spent his days writing "leftist" essays that not only supported the Communist Party but demanded more rigorous party rule in China. Since Lu Jiaping was not adept with computers he had his son Hu post them on his Web site.[147]

Liu Di, a young psychology student and Internet enthusiast, was arrested on the campus of Beijing University on November 7, 2002, on the eve of the opening of the 16th Congress of the Chinese Communist Party, and was held in an undisclosed location. She was one of the most famous Internet web-masters in China, known by her cyber *nom de plume*, the "stainless-steel mouse." Ms. Liu wrote absurdist essays in the style of dissident Eastern-bloc writers of the 1970s and ran a popular web-posting site. Admirers cite her originality and humor. In one essay, she asserted that China's repressive national security laws were not good for the security of the nation. It was months before Liu was heard from since her secret arrest. No charges were filed against her; her family and friends were not permitted to visit her; and, in a well-known silencing tactic, authorities warned that it would not go well for her if foreign media were informed of her case.[148] Not until a year later, on November 28, 2003 was Liu Di released on bail.

In December 2002, *The New York Times* reported on a study by Harvard Law School researchers, which found that China had the most extensive and effective Internet censorship in the world. It regularly denies local users access to 19,000 Web sites that the government deems threatening.[149] The study, which tested access from multiple points in China over six months, found that Beijing blocked thousands of the most popular news, political and religious sites, along with selected entertainment and educational destinations.[150] The researchers said censors sometimes punished people who sought forbidden information by temporarily making it hard for them to gain any access to the Internet.

Defying predictions that the Internet was inherently too diverse and malleable for state control, China has denied a vast majority of its 46 million Internet users access to information that it feels could weaken its authoritarian power. Beijing only allows Internet use for commercial, entertainment and other purposes, which it views as essential in a globalized era.* Only the most determined and technologically savvy users can evade the Chinese censorship filtering, and they do so at some personal risk, the Harvard study says. "If the purpose of such filtering is to influence what the average Chinese Internet user sees, success could be within grasp," said Jonathan Zittrain, a professor at the law school and a co-author of the study.

Beijing completely blocks access to the major sites on Tibet, Taiwan or democracy study and advocacy organizations. Chinese users cannot often reach the sites run by Amnesty International or Human Rights Watch. China also does not allow users to connect to major Western religious sites. News media sites are also often blocked. China claims its main

* Strangely enough, China has become "the headquarters of choice" for many spammers according to Spamhaus Project one of the most effective activist groups fighting unwanted e-mails (Saul Hansell, "Spammers Can Run But They Cant Hide," *The New York Times*, November 9, 2003).

justification for censorship is the proliferation of pornography. Yet the study found that China blocked fewer than 15 percent of the most popular sexually explicit sites. Saudi Arabia banned 86 percent of the list.

In September 2002, reports began to appear that the Chinese government had blocked its citizens from using the popular search-engine Google.[151] Chinese seeking access to Google were seamlessly rerouted to sites that were registered with Chinese authorities and complied with Beijing's rules to filter content for Chinese users.

The contrast between such officially approved search engines (one of which is Yahoo) and Google is stark. A search for information related to Jiang Zemin on Google turned up 154,000 references. The first was a link to a site run by Falun Gong and bitterly critical of Jiang. An identical search on Yahoo produced just six references. The first one was the "Life Story of President Jiang Zemin" written by the *People's Daily*, the voice of the Chinese Communist Party. *Beijing Legal Times* reported that Google was shut down because it contained "harmful content."

A computer science student at the University of Toronto, Nart Villeneuve, has created a program he calls a "pseudoproxy" that would enable Chinese Internet users to gain access to Google through an unblocked look-alike site.[152] Internet groups such as the Freenet China Project are working on this and other solutions to fight China's Internet censorship. These efforts have yet to make any discernable impression on the Chinese government's increasingly repressive policies in this regard.

On June 26, 2004, a Chinese court announced that an Internet commentator, Du Daobin, who had earlier been charged with subversion, would get a suspended sentence instead of a long prison term. Mr. Du had been arrested for speaking out against the jailing of Liu Di, the "stainless steel mouse." Though human rights groups, who had raised an outcry about Du's arrest, applauded what seemed like an official show of leniency, many Internet commentators in China "are warning that what appears to be government magnanimity in this high-profile case conceals a quiet but concerted push to tighten controls of the Internet and surveillance of its users even though China's restrictions on the medium are already among the broadest and most invasive anywhere."[153]

"The average Internet user (in China), meanwhile, neither sees nor, in many cases, suspects the activities of a force widely estimated to number as many as 30,000 Internet police officers...The Chinese government has also established a Web site where people are able to report fellow Web users for suspicious or provocative behavior."[154]

A recent *BBC* report from Beijing stated that China was expanding its censorship controls to cover text messages sent using mobile phones. New regulations have been issued to allow mobile phone companies to police and filter messages. Analysts fear the real targets are political dissidents. A Paris-based group, Reporters Without Borders, says the Chinese authorities are increasingly using new technology to control information. One Chinese company marketing a system to monitor mobile phone text messages has announced it is watching for "false political rumours" and "reactionary remarks." Certain key words could trigger an automatic alert to the police.

Text messaging has already threatened Beijing's control over information. Last year, the authorities tried to hide the outbreak of the respiratory disease SARS. But millions of text messages were sent, alerting people to the virus and exposing the government cover-up. So far only China Mobile Corporation has used the regulation, but seeing that it controls

65 percent of the mobile phone market "... these new rules will almost certainly become the industry standard."[155]

U.S. technology firms have aided in the erection of the Chinese government's cyber barrier. "Prominent American corporations, including Cisco Systems, Microsoft, Nortel Networks, Websense and Sun Microsystems, have all played a part in quickly equipping China with censoring equipment," Jill R. Newbold writes in the *Journal of Law, Technology and Policy*, published by the University of Illinois at Urbana-Champaign. Newbold also asserts that American Tech companies and Internet Service Providers have had to sign a Chinese government public pledge not to produce, post or disseminate information that "may jeopardize state security and disrupt social stability" on pain of losing their state licenses to operate. Newbold argues that the rule has made American institutions complicit in China's cyber censorship. More than 300 corporations, government agencies and universities have signed these agreements, which "throws the Web principles of free speech and access to open information out the window."[156]

World's Largest Supplier of Nuclear Weapons to Rogue States

Before September 11, 2001, there was no doubt in the mind of US intelligence agencies of China's major, if not preeminent, role in the global proliferation of Weapons of Mass Destruction. A CIA report stated that "during the last half of 1996, China was the most significant supplier of Weapons of Mass Destruction related goods and technology to foreign countries."[157] The American Office of Naval Intelligence maintained that the flow of materials and technology from China to Iran was "one of the most active 'Weapons of Mass Destruction' programs in the third world."[158] Chinese arms companies were also deeply engaged in Iraq.

On February 22, 2001, President Bush announced that the U.S. knew that China was involved in developing electronics and radar systems in Iraq to be used against American and British warplanes; an allegation that China was not completely able to deny.[159] In an earlier address on national defense (at the Citadel in Charleston, S.C. on September 23, 1999), Bush spelled out this oblique warning of China's nuclear threat: "In 1996, after some tension over Taiwan, a Chinese general reminded America that China possesses the means to incinerate Los Angeles with nuclear missiles."[160]

In light of the flap about President Bush and Prime Minister Blair's misrepresentations about Iraq's purchase of uranium ore from Niger, it may help to redirect public perception to the real problem of nuclear proliferation, by pointing out that, unlike the uranium from Niger, there is no controversy among WMD experts about the source of the blueprint plans for Iraq's once projected nuclear device. This was, in fact, a tested Chinese design that had also been used successfully by Pakistan.[161]

Pakistan's nuclear weapon program was secretly launched in 1972. A *New York Times* report describes China's vital contribution to the genesis of the first "Islamic bomb."* "China, a staunch ally of Pakistan's, provided blueprints for the bomb, as well as highly enriched uranium, tritium, scientists and key components for a nuclear weapons production complex, among other crucial tools. 'Without China's help, Pakistan's bomb would not exist' said Gary Milhollin, a leading expert on the spread of nuclear weapons."[162] Pakistan's program also relied on clandestine acquisition of nuclear technology from the Netherlands, Germany and even from the United States.

According to one of the latest surveys of WMD proliferation published by the Carnegie Endowment for International Peace,** "China's assistance to Pakistan's nuclear program over the past 15 years may have been critical to Pakistan's nuclear weapon breakthroughs in the 1980s. China was believed to have supplied Pakistan with the plans for one of its earlier nuclear bombs and possibly to have provided enough highly enriched uranium for two such weapons."[163] The Carnegie Endowment-supported survey also details China's assistance to

* The term "Islamic bomb" was first coined by a former prime minister of Pakistan, Zulfikar Ali Bhutto, and is what most people in Pakistan now proudly call their nation's nuclear arsenal. Pakistani officials, aware of the term's negative connotation in the West, object to its use.

** Recently the Carnegie Endowment came into the media spotlight for issuing a detailed report on the Bush administration's hyping of Iraq's WMD capabilities.

Pakistan in the construction of a plutonium production reactor at Khusab and an un-safeguarded plutonium reprocessing facility at Chasma, giving Pakistan, for the first time, a dependable source of plutonium for use in nuclear weapons.

Though China has consistently claimed that it does not help other countries to develop nuclear weapons, the Clinton administration accused China, in August 1995, of selling 5,000 ring magnets the previous year to Pakistan. The custom-built ring magnets, made of an advanced samarium-cobalt alloy, enabled Pakistan to upgrade and replace its uranium enrichment centrifuges.[164]

There is also the disturbing trail of evidence pointing to the possible links between Pakistan's nuclear program and Al Qaeda.* Seymour Hersh, the investigative journalist for the *New Yorker*, was told by an American nonproliferation expert, "Right now, the most dangerous country in the world is Pakistan. If we're incinerated next week, it'll be because of H.E.U – highly enriched uranium – that was given to Al Qaeda by Pakistan."[165]

In the last few years, a trail of evidence, circumstantial yet fairly damning, has been uncovered relating to China's indirect and highly secretive involvement in the development of North Korea's nuclear weapons program. In June 2002, the CIA delivered a comprehensive analysis of North Korea's nuclear

---

* In the weeks before Sept. 11, a 38-year veteran of Pakistan's nuclear program, Sultan Bashiruddin Mahmood, was discovered to have visited Osama bin Laden at least twice in Afghanistan, where the two are reported to have discussed nuclear weapons ("In Pakistan, U.S. Embraces Friend of a Foe," *The New York Times*, May 25, 2002). After the American arrival in Afghanistan, three top nuclear scientists with close ties to Al Qaeda and the Taliban, Mizra Yusuf Baig, Chaudhury Abdul Majid and our earlier-mentioned Sultan Bashiruddin Mahmood, were, at the behest of American intelligence, taken in for "questioning" but were subsequently released ("The Cold Test: What the Administration knew about Pakistan and the North Korean nuclear program," Seymour M. Hersh, *The New Yorker*, January 27, 2003).

ambitions to President Bush and his top advisors. "The documents' most politically sensitive information, however, was about Pakistan. Since 1997, the CIA said, Pakistan had been sharing sophisticated technology, warhead-design information, and weapons-testing data with the Pyongyang regime. Pakistan, one of the Bush Administration's important allies in the war against terrorism and chief recipient of Chinese nuclear technology, was helping North Korea build the bomb."[166] The Bush administration even imposed sanctions against a major Pakistani nuclear laboratory – the first such action since Pakistan became an ally in the battle against terrorism.[167] The father of Pakistan's nuclear bomb, A.Q. Khan, is known to have paid at least 13 visits to North Korea.[168]

In return, Pakistan received nuclear-capable ballistic missiles and delivery systems technology from North Korea. The barter-trade between the two countries was spelled out to members of Congress by the CIA in November 2002.[169] Yet, somehow, the fundamental fact of the Chinese origins of both Pakistan's nuclear technology and North Korea's missile technology was completely overlooked in all the reports, and even escaped the notice of every media story on the issue.

There is also little doubt that China approved the barter deal, even if it may not have been involved in setting it up. When the "nuclear barter" story broke out in the international media, China did not bother to direct even the mildest of censure to any of the two parties who were in effect trading weapons and technology that China had originally supplied to them. In fact, there was not even a momentary pause in China's military assistance program to Pakistan, which is extensive and vital to Pakistan's survival. North Korea, which is near totally dependent on China for military assistance and even energy and food, did not see any lessening of support. China has in effect devised a clever shell-game — "now you see it now you don't" — where it can move nuclear weapons and delivery systems through these proxy nations with complete deniability.

This shell-game also permits China to implement a hitherto unheard of "nuclear-threat-by-proxy" strategy, giving it a substantial advantage over its adversaries in military and geopolitical terms. For instance, by building up Pakistan's nuclear arsenal and missile systems, China has effectively checkmated India and blind-sided India's growing challenge as China's main Asian rival.[170] The strategy further allows China to deliver a genuine nuclear threat to its enemies, while appearing to the world at large to remain above the fray. Of course, the victim is often aware of the origin of the threat but lacks direct evidence to register a convincing protest.

On August 31, 1998, North Korea launched the nuclear-capable Taepo Dong-I three-stage intermediate range ballistic missile. As this "rivet for rivet" clone of China's CSS-2 missile roared over Japan's northernmost island on it first test flight, Japan awoke to find that its security assumptions had suddenly and radically changed, and not for the better. It did not take much time for the unwelcome conclusion to sink in that the missile test was actually a statement by proxy from Beijing: that China was now the big power in East Asia and Japan's position as the effective platform for U.S. power projection in the region would not be accepted without a challenge. That the missile test was, as intended, seen by most Japanese as a message from China, is clear from the responses that came afterwards. An opposition leader, Ichiro Ozawa declared that "…if China gets too inflated, the Japanese people will become hysterical. We have plenty of plutonium in our nuclear power plants, so it's possible for us to produce 3,000 to 4,000 nuclear warheads." Doubts about American guarantees to defend Japan were not lagging far behind. Taro Kono, a member of Parliament said: "Simply put, we doubt that the United States would sacrifice Los Angeles for Tokyo."[171]

North Korea's recent belligerent announcements of the success of its nuclear weapons program and its ability to soon make a small arsenal of nuclear bombs has forced the Bush administration to perform a very ungraceful about-turn in its China policy. All previous statements from the Bush administration of China being a nuclear threat or of it being the most significant supplier of Weapons of Mass Destruction-related goods and technology to foreign countries have not only vanished but no hint has been raised anywhere in the American administration, Congress, or even the media of China's responsibility in the creation of North Korea's nuclear threat in the first place.

Furthermore, it has given Beijing the opportunity to assume the moral high ground and set itself up as an honest broker between the USA and North Korea.* After a first somewhat fruitless round of meetings, China vociferously called for a next round of talks between the USA and North Korea and assigned to itself an assertive mediating role in the proceedings.[172] America, mired in Iraq and at odds with its traditional allies, was in no position to refuse. Even when in August of 2003 an unlikely combination of American manufacturers, labor leaders and

---

* China, of course, did the same earlier with the Clinton administration. According to the diplomatic correspondent for the *Los Angeles Times*, James Mann, "The Chinese may also have been making use of the North Korean nuclear dispute as a way of demonstrating their importance to the United States. The timing of their effort in Pyongyang was remarkable. In early June 1994, just two weeks after Clinton announced he would extend China's most-favored-nation benefits, the Chinese for the first time told North Korea that China might go along with a United Nations resolution imposing sanctions against Pyongyang. Within a few days, President Kim Il Sung agreed to freeze his country's nuclear program" (*About Face: A History of America's Curious Relationship with China, From Nixon to Clinton*, James Mann, Knopf, 1999).

both Republican and Democratic congressmen called on the President to stand up against China's unfair export practices, which were costing the USA a huge number of job losses and loss of manufacturing, the Bush administration's first priority was not to offend China.[173] In fact, China's involvement has come as such a relief to everyone that despite lack of evidence, media accounts of the problem these days tend to highlight China's exasperation with North Korea and its success in arm-twisting its junior partner to the negotiating table. No suggestion has ever been raised that this could all be, even if only in part, skillful diplomatic theatre.

The latest three-day summit took place on August 27, 2003 in Beijing with Russia, Japan, and South Korea participating as well. The meeting concluded with absolutely no progress on any issue, except for an agreement on a next round of talks. On the second day of the conference, North Korea's chief delegate, Kim Yong Il, startled the other negotiators when he declared that his country "had developed nuclear weapons and was prepared to prove that it could successfully deliver and explode them."[174] In another shock to the Americans, the Chinese official, Wang Yi, who played host to the six-party talks said, "the United States was the 'main problem' in reaching a diplomatic solution to the crisis, echoing the North's (Korea) bitter assessment about why the talks had ended in acrimony."[175]

Recently, in January 2004, *The New York Times* published two front-page stories detailing Pakistan's peddling of "advanced nuclear technology" to Libya, North Korea and even Iran.[176] The story followed the decision by Libyan leader Muammar Gadaffi to renounce Weapons of Mass Destruction and open his country's weapons laboratories to international inspection.

Then on February 17, 2004, the *Washington Post* came out with the story that Libya's nuclear weapon design had come from

China. The discovery was made by international inspectors after they studied a package of documents turned over to U.S. officials in November last year by Libyan authorities. "The bomb designs and other papers turned over by Libya have yielded dramatic evidence of China's long-suspected role in transferring nuclear know-how to Pakistan." The *Post* story also mentioned that "the packet of documents, some of which included text in Chinese, contained detailed, step-by-step instructions for assembling an implosion-type nuclear bomb that could fit atop a large ballistic missile. They also included technical instructions for manufacturing components for the device, the officials and experts said."[177]

China's actions "were irresponsible and short-sighted, and raise questions about what else China provided to Pakistan's nuclear program,"[178] said David Albright, a nuclear physicist and former U.N. weapons inspector in Iraq. Though it would have been pertinent to the issue, Albright did not mention the fact that the bomb design for Iraq's aborted nuclear weapons program had also been of Chinese origin.[179]

On June 15, 2004, *Reuters* reported that congressional investigators from the US-China Economic and Security Review Commission had accused China of sending nuclear technology to Iran in exchange for oil and allowing North Korea to use Chinese air, rail and seaports to ship missiles and other weapons. "China's assistance to weapons of mass destruction-related programs in countries of concern continues, despite repeated promises to end such activities and the repeated imposition of U.S. sanctions," the commission concluded. This "calls into question the effectiveness" of Washington's partnership with Beijing, the panel said.[180]

Sun Tzu said that all strategy was based on deception. If one looks at the whole thing dispassionately, perhaps as a high-stakes chess tournament, one can only marvel at the skill and patience with which China has consistently outmaneuvered all its opponents. But when we must add to the equation the cold-blooded cynicism with which China has provided nuclear weapons and delivery systems to despotic and dangerous regimes, creating the possibility of near-imminent nuclear conflict in South Asia and North East Asia, and furthermore made possible the passage of nuclear weapons into the hands of Islamic terrorists,* admiration must surely give way to dismay and condemnation.

* In his most recent book, *Qui A Tué Daniel Pearl?* (*Who Killed Daniel Pearl?*, Melville House, 2003), France's leading philosopher Bernard Henri Lévy, who undertook a personal investigation of Islamic terrorism in Pakistan, Britain, Bosnia and India, convincingly argues that "Al Qaeda is largely controlled by the Pakistani secret service" and that "the Pakistani atomic bomb was built and is controlled by radical Islamists who intend to use it someday."

China Does Not Play by the Usual Rules of Business

Of course, developed nations calling for free trade and globalization often do not practice what they preach. But even taking into account unfair American and European trade practices (subsidies to farmers, etc.), there is growing awareness that China's disregard for the usual rules of business is altogether in a class all by itself.

Protectionism in China is a gigantic and unimaginably complicated system, featuring not only the standard state subsidies of exports industries, but a host of practices designed not only to undercut competitive foreign-made goods but to confuse Western businessmen and politicians intending to overcome it. Another method is import substitution. The Chinese government rigs the market so that items being imported are produced domestically even if the cost is greater. One U.S. government report catalogued the bewildering array of devices that China employs to block imports from the U.S. and other countries: prohibitively high tariffs, import licenses, import quotas, import restrictions and certification requirements. In some cases, after pressure from the U.S. Congress or some federal agency, Chinese trade bureaucrats removed barriers on imports with great fanfare while simultaneously but quietly installing new barriers against the same imports.[181]

China's entry into the WTO was supposed to make its business practices more transparent and accountable, but there is little evidence of any fundamental change taking place. We read of new laws being enacted in China to facilitate commerce and finance and even protect intellectual property and the rights of foreign investors, but as long as the legal system in China is merely a compliant tool of the government and the Communist party, then nothing really changes.

Furthermore, American trade policies and the policies of such federal agencies as the Export-Import Bank have had the perverse effect of sending American jobs overseas. A major Chinese steel company received an $18 million loan in December 2000 to buy American-made equipment only to be found a year later dumping steel into American markets, in a year steel companies in the United States had laid off 30,000 workers and more than 20 of the companies filed for bankruptcy.[182]

The same Export-Import Bank recently refused a major loan to Aaron Feuerstein, the 77-year-old chairman of Malden Mills, makers of Polartec Fleece, to save his company.[183] Readers may recall the heartwarming news and feature stories in the winter of 1995/96 of how, after a disastrous fire in his mill in Lawrence, Massachusetts, Mr. Feuerstein did not take the insurance money and relocate his factory to China. What was even more remarkable, he continued to pay his thousands of idled workers — whose families were dependent on his factory — for the months that passed ($25 million in total) till he had rebuilt his mill in Lawrence. Aaron Feuerstein received international acclaim, numerous awards of every kind, and was invited to the White House by President Clinton. His company is now bankrupt.

Economists who argue that though such traditional industries as steel or textile may lose out to China, America has an overwhelming advantage in such areas as entertainment and hi-tech should reevaluate their information. A report in *The New*

York Times, in August 2003, stated that the Motion Picture Association of America estimated that last year more than 90 percent of DVD's sold in China were pirated copies, and that the film piracy in the Asia-Pacific region cost filmmakers $640 million in foregone sales, with China the top violator.[184] Furthermore, the International Federation of the Phonograph Industry recently estimated that more than 90 percent of all music CD's sold in China last year were pirated copies, costing the business $530 million in lost sales. Even many of the pirated DVDs and CDs sold on the streets of New York and Los Angeles have been made in China.

Besides DVD and CD piracy there is the counterfeiting of nearly every Western and Japanese manufactured product and design. The CBS television program *60 Minutes II* raised this issue in January 2004 and this is what they had to say about the problem: "Name an American brand. Any brand, and any kind of product. Clothing, computer chips, car parts. Just name it and we'll tell you something about it. It's probably being counterfeited in China, right now, as we speak. For years, China has been the workshop of the world. And for years, American and other western firms have set up shop in China to tap into the enormous, cheap labor force. The question is — once the Chinese know how to make an American product, what's to stop them from copying it? The answer? Nothing at all. And what's to prevent the Chinese from shipping these counterfeits back to the United States? Not much, reports correspondent Bob Simon."[185]

"We have never seen a problem of this size and magnitude in world history. There's more counterfeiting going on in China now than we've ever seen anywhere," says Dan Chow, a law professor at Ohio State University who specializes in Chinese counterfeiting."[186]

According to a *New York Times* business report of January 2004, China is fast gaining in technology and poses significant trade worries for the West. For instance, the Chinese government announced in December 2003 that foreign computer and chip makers that want to sell wireless devices in China would have to use Chinese encryption software and co-produce their goods with a designated list of Chinese companies. International corporations are worried not only about the creation of separate technical standards but also the possible loss of intellectual property if they are forced to work with Chinese companies that could become future competitors.

In the matter of the next generation of DVDs, which hold four to five times the data of current discs, the Chinese standard, called EVD, appears to be "more an escape hatch around the patent pools of the established companies than a technology breakthrough," said Richard Doherty, president of the Envisioneering Group, a technology consulting firm.[187] Essentially this appears to be an effort to avoid hefty royalty payments to patent-holding companies in Japan, USA and Europe. But since about half of the world's DVD players are now made in China, there is every possibility that China could force through international acceptance of its EVD standard.

To appreciate the true significance of this development we should cast our minds back to the seventies and eighties when businessmen, lobbyists and politicians were selling their vision of China as the world's largest untapped market for Western consumer goods. "If we could sell only one TV (or one wrist-watch, or even one bar of soap) to every Chinese…." was the constant and now familiar refrain of that early period of the China trade. In 1984, the chairman of IBM, Ralph A. Pfeiffer Jr., happily mused to the American press, "If we could sell one IBM PC for every hundred people in China, or every 1,000, or even every 10,000…"[188] He left the sentence unfinished. Now China is not only selling the world nearly every consumer good imaginable (including PCs and components), acquired most of the factories that were making them all in the first place, hijacked every kind of technology (including sensitive military ones), but has even begun to make moves on the intellectual properties behind the technology and creative resources of the developed world.

Probably the best exposé on the perils of doing business in China came out a few years ago from one of the most respected experts in this field. Joe Studwell has been a contributing editor to *The Economist* as well as several other international business publications and has covered foreign investment in China for *The Economist Intelligence Unit.* He is also the founder and editor-in-chief of the *China Economic Quarterly.* He lived in China from 1990 to 2000. His book, *The China Dream,* details the incredible amount of hype about China's economic market.[189] Its huge population, high-skilled, low-wage work force, and relative political stability for a developing country all act as a powerful lure to multinationals eager to set up shop and begin selling to one-quarter of the world's population. Under tough negotiations from Chinese officials, these companies tend to give away the kitchen sink to ensure they get access to the huge market. But what do they get in return?

Studwell does a service to the informed public by clearly demonstrating that almost all the businesses that have gone to China have gotten next to nothing for their technology transfers, special fees and tremendous time and effort they've dedicated to the market. Almost uniformly, they have high-balled their expected sales and profits from the Middle Kingdom and found immense barriers such as unseen regulations and fees, corrupt officials, un-enforced laws, local spin-offs to their products, etc. that should have sent them packing. Yet almost all of them push on, undeterred. As Studwell explains, the reason for this is an old phenomenon among Western businessmen that goes back to the eighteenth century and which he calls "The China Dream." Despite continual setbacks, these hard-headed businessmen are too attracted to the possibility that they have something to sell that even a small percentage of Chinese may want to buy. Those huge potential numbers are too much of an enticement to businesses to easily let go of their foothold in China.

Studwell's book, though published in 2002, has managed to maintain a remarkable relevance right up to the present moment. The March 20-26, 2004 issue of *The Economist* carried a detailed twenty-page survey of "Business In China," which virtually repeated all the salient arguments made in *The China Dream* (including Studwell's history lesson as to the origins of the "dream") with only some updating of certain statistics and information.

But Studwell's book is more than just about the experience of foreign businessmen in China. It also shows that the China market is becoming a trap for the Chinese people themselves. They work hard and save and the government in effect confiscates and then destroys their money by trapping it in state-owned banks that are insolvent because they lend to state-owned enterprises that are unproductive. This is not the place to go into a lengthy discussion on China's banking problems but for those who would like to read more on the subject a list of relevant articles is provided in this particular citation.[190]

One of the articles in the above citation is a review of a serious economic tome *Zhongguo de xianjing (China's Pitfall)* by He Qingliang. This, according to Jonathan Mirsky, is the first systematic study of the social consequences of China's economic "boom," which according to He Qingliang amounted from the outset "to a process in which power-holders and their hangers-on plundered public wealth." The book published in Hong Kong and Beijing became a huge bestseller (pirated in five separate editions) and subsequently led to her persecution by officialdom.

She managed to flee to the USA in 2002. He Qingliang tell us that the Chinese official figures maintain that 20 percent of loans given out by China's banks are "non-performing" (i.e., never repaid) but the actual figure may be between 40 and 60 percent. International banks observe a bad debt ratio of under three percent. Even five years after the publication of He's book, the Chinese government does not seem to have put adequate reforms into place. A *New York Times* report of November 6, 2003, mentions that international credit rating agencies were concerned that China's banks would need a major bail out because of non-performing loans.[191]

The caption on a more recent *New York Times* (December 2003) article asks, "Is the Chinese Economy a Bubble in the Making?" The report goes on to describe how a "dysfunctional banking system," and short-sighted "let the good times roll" policies were creating an overheated economy where "so many steel mills are being built there that all the world's iron ore mines together may not be able to supply them."[192] A more detailed article, "Is China The Next Bubble?," warning of a "Southeast Asian Miracle" style bust appeared in January 2004.[193] The article also discussed the political instability that could follow such an event.

With China's economic policies showing a "strong inclination to let the good times roll for now and to worry later about any ensuing bust" there is certainly fast money to be made, though for the outsider such prospects appear to be largely confined to the export sector. For a Western businessperson this opportunity can be availed by relocating his or her manufacturing base to China, participating in the cold-hearted but profitable exploitation of China's helpless migrant labor force, and actively contributing to the unemployment and soaring trade deficit figures in his or her own country.

On the subject of deficits: the last half-decade has seen a series of dramatically rising annual trade deficit figures in the U.S., especially in relation to China. According to the Economic Policy Institute, "China's trade surplus with the United States increased 20 percent in 2003 to $124 billion. The U.S. trade deficit with China is now the largest it has with any country in the world. Imports from China are now 5.7 times the value of U.S. exports to China, making it the United States' most imbalanced trading relationship."[194]

In the case of Japan, the U.S. balance of payment climbed slowly for three decades till it began falling in the mid-nineties. With China it seems to have struck almost overnight. In the entire postwar history of trade competition, by contrast, Japan never came close to putting the United States in such a disadvantageous position. Yet we might recall the Japan phobia that affected America in the eighties, exemplified by Michael Crichton's novel and the film, *Rising Sun.* Despite the vigorous trade competition, Japan was only a small, peaceful island nation, a democracy and a particularly close ally of the USA — a near client state as far as defense was concerned. It should also be borne in mind that Japan's exports were genuinely the product of the nation's technological and manufacturing excellence and that Japanese workers not only received fair wages but an unheard of "lifetime employment."

China is not only the world's most populous nation, but one that is avowedly hostile to democracy in general and the United States in particular. It is also, unlike Japan, a nuclear power that is everyday increasing its military power and aggressively pursuing an expansionist policy. China's export success is not the result of indigenous creativity and manufacturing excellence, but essentially the result of the heartless exploitation of a desperate, disenfranchised and near-enslaved labor force by a cynical government and piratical international corporations.

In the long haul though, lost profits and deficit figures might possibly matter a bit less than the steady undermining of the whole democratic/capitalist structure on which Western prosperity and security rests. According to William Safire, this is happening by the successful propagation of the notion that capitalist prosperity can be successfully abetted by political repression. Safire in his column in *The New York Times* described this as "the Singapore virus,"[195] which he felt could infect the global economy with its strain of fascism.

This clean, orderly world of a single political party, an effectively muzzled but entertaining modern media, docile rubber-stamp judges, disenfranchised labor, decent golf courses and fat profits for the business and political elite is not without its enthusiasts and advocates in the West. Henry Kissinger, James Schlessinger and other members of the Nixon Center for Peace and Prosperity have honored Singapore's former boss, Lee Kuan Yew ("Hitler with a heart") as "architect of the next century." For sometime in the eighties and nineties, China regarded Singapore as the model for its economic and social development. These days the pupil has outstripped the master and the same sort of praise once lavished on Singapore is now being heaped on China – and by the very same people. At the same time, the China/Singapore admiration club has expanded and now includes those not so obviously on the Republican right as Fareed Zakaria, editor of *Newsweek International*, as mentioned in the introduction, Nicholas Kristof, columnist for *The New York Times*, and others.

The latest entrant to the club is Robert Mugabe, president (for life?) of Zimbabwe. Underscoring his rejection of democracy and the West, Mugabe, in a state-of-the-nation address to parliament on December 2, 2003, said China was increasingly becoming "an alternative global power point" indicating "a new alternative direction, which in fact could be the foundation of a new global paradigm."[196] A recent report in *Commentary* reveals a growing movement in Saudi Arabia towards China as a partner, "paradigm" and principal ally, as China's booming economy becomes ever more dependent on Middle Eastern Oil and Saudi-American relations become increasingly strained.[197]

With the fall of the Berlin Wall there was a brief period in world history when it appeared that not only had Western capitalist democracy triumphed decisively, but that no possible alternatives even existed to it anymore. We may recall the hubristic declarations about "The End of History" and the like that were characteristic of those heady days. Yet, *pace* Francis Fukuyama, history not only does not end but sometimes repeats itself, too often in unfortunate ways. We could now be seeing the beginning of an era, quite similar to the years between the two World Wars, when intellectuals, politicians and plutocrats worldwide caviled against the restraints and perceived limitations of democratic governance and sought more profitable and inspiring alternatives in the doctrines of Hitler and Mussolini. Perhaps such a reading could be regarded as unduly alarmist, but China's conscious and perhaps even calculated metamorphosis to a fascist (the term is used in a technical non-pejorative sense) state and paradigm, has not entirely escaped the attention of experts in the field (see pages 113-115).

At the moment many Americans of both liberal and conservative stripe are rightly concerned about the erosion of fundamental civil liberties in the US in the wake of the Bush administration's "War on Terror." Though 9/11 was certainly of portentous significance in this respect, it might more accurately be viewed as one moment, albeit a very important one, in the long course of the cynical undermining of human freedom that has been going on for sometime now. A smaller but yet significant milestone in this process might include Bill Clinton's de-linking of human rights and the China trade, while the oft-repeated and self-serving statements of business leaders and politicians that democracy was unsuited to Chinese cultural values, that human rights were overrated, and the general silence of intellectuals and the public on these issues, certainly provided the requisite *mise en scène* of expedient acquiescence.

In the end, the object lesson Americans may derive from this period in their history is that when you fail to speak up for the freedom of others, you embolden those who want to take yours away.

Conclusion

So much of what we read these days has the net effect of making us feel helpless and frustrated. If this book has succeeded in upsetting you or better still aroused in you unmanageable feelings of indignation and outrage, then rest assured that you can do something about it — right now, today, and every day after that, if you like. In addition, what you will be doing will be direct, absolutely legal and non-violent in a hands-on Gandhian way. Just undertake a personal boycott of "Made in China" products.

If experience serves, the moment you even consider such a course of action a host of (quite plausible sounding) reasons to back out will start gnawing away at your resolution. How can my individual boycott possibly have any impact on the booming economy of the world's most populous country? Does a boycott make economic sense? Will it hurt or help the Chinese people? Read the subsequent Q&A section where answers to, and discussions on, most, if not all, of your questions are provided.

If after that you are convinced that a personal boycott is a good idea you could check the website of the *Boycott Made In China* Campaign at www.boycottmadeinchina.org for various reference and publicity materials, advice on going about a boycott, links to various organizations and so on. You might also consider joining the campaign.

The *Boycott Made in China* Campaign represents a worldwide coalition of Tibetan organizations, Tibet support groups, Chinese dissident groups, human rights and other activist groups. The campaign itself was launched on Saturday, December 7, 2002. The date was selected to honor Human Rights Day (December 10th).

To date nearly a hundred organizations have endorsed the boycott campaign and individuals from all around the world have pledged not to buy any products manufactured in the People's Republic of China. The campaign now has active boycotters in Côte de Ivoire, Argentina, Japan, Norway, Switzerland, Spain, Ghana, Australia, the Czech Republic, Venezuela, Brazil, India, New Zealand, the Philippines, Britain, Scotland, Germany, France, Canada and the United States.

In spite of the satisfying list of country names, the campaign is admittedly a small one at the moment. Furthermore, the individual-based, non-violent method chosen will, because of its inherent grass-roots nature, require some time to deliver results. Yet, this drawback is more than compensated for by the fact that it is a strategy that does not depend for its success on the goodwill or intercession of politicians and businessmen — people who are most susceptible to China's economic blandishments. It also keeps the movement out of the clutches of the all-powerful China lobby in Washington, D.C. (operating from the Boeing office) which has a near perfect record of subverting the efforts of human rights, labor, religious and Tibetan lobby groups calling for trade restrictions of any kind with China.

The individual boycott route does not require complex organization or substantial funding for its success. Essentially, all it requires is for you not to buy "Made in China" products. When enough of you do that, and when one day a critical mass of humanity-of-conscience thus acts together, then the collective power of its moral outrage should not only shake our own leaders from their apathy and cynicism, but possibly bring about a dramatic and humanizing change in the Communist/Fascist regime in Beijing.

Clearing Remaining Doubts Q&A

Nearly all the questions listed here actually came up at one time or the other in discussions with Tibetan activists and Tibet supporters, hence the various references to Tibet and Tibetan activism.

Q. I have been reading that China is moving towards democracy. Won't a boycott of Chinese products impact negatively on this progress?

A. Optimistic reports of slow but steady progress towards democratic governance in China are, in the main, based on self-serving analysis or outright wishful thinking. One "proof" usually offered of China's democratization is the decision in 2002 by the Chinese Communist Party (CCP) to include businessmen into its ranks. What that has accomplished according to a *New York Times* report on the 16th Party Congress in Beijing by Joseph Kahn has been "to transform the world's last major left-wing dictatorship into the world's last major right-wing dictatorship."[198] Furthermore, what many reports failed to point out was that nearly all the leading financial, business and industrial figures in China were invariably the close relatives, sons, daughters, nephews, wives, etc., of China's highest-ranking Communist Party officials.

The New York Times also printed an Op-Ed on the 16th Congress by Bao Tong, the highest party official imprisoned for opposing the Tiananmen Square crackdown now released but living under constant police surveillance. Mr. Tong declared that it would be "irrational" to think that China was moving in the direction of democracy. He asks: "What difference does it make if older authoritarians are replaced by younger, technically trained or even capitalist authoritarians? Not much."[199]

Jasper Becker has published a detailed analysis of China's political metamorphosis in a recent article. This is his theory on the genesis of this transformation: "Realizing that the demise of communism deprived the CCP of an ideology and a reason to exist, Jiang (Zemin), Hu (Jintao), and their peers are quietly remaking China into a fascist state bearing a striking resemblance to its '20s predecessors... the kind of highly nationalistic right-wing dictatorship that emerged in the '20s and '30s in Germany, Spain, Japan, Romania, and most notably Italy. Since at least the late '80s CCP leaders have instituted economic programs recalling fascist ideas of "planned capitalism." To complement its economic policies, the CCP has developed a neo-fascist political program of mass rallies, nationalist indoctrination, and party control over private lives."[200]

Whether change from Communism to Fascism can be regarded as an improvement is, of course, a matter of one's political inclination, but it certainly cannot be considered a step towards democracy. China has not met even the minimum of requirements to qualify for acceptance as a democracy, even on the somewhat dubious level of Robert Mugabe's Zimbabwe, which has a parliament and an opposition party, though a much harried one. There is a bottom line in these things as Jasper Becker points out: "China is now one of the last countries in the world without a functioning parliament. The National People's Congress does exist but it has no building of its own, no permanent staff or offices, and it assembles for just ten days a year. During the rest of the year only members of the Standing Committee, which is made up entirely of senior Party officials, meet."[201]

Even the uncomplimentary label of "debating society" usually attached to toothless assemblies or powerless political organizations, cannot be applied to China's Congress, as no debates of any kind are tolerated from the members of that body. A Western correspondent at the Party Congress reported that the discussions sounded like recitations and the main speech of the president "was notable mostly for its vagueness." He mentioned further that "...the 2,114 people chosen to decide the party's future at this congress are not debating those issues (who's going to rule). Instead, they met this weekend in small groups, sat in places assigned to them based on rank, and read from reports that expressed fealty to senior party leaders."[202]

A clear indication of China's steady regression into anti-democratic authoritarianism is evident in its premeditated step-by-step campaign to undermine Hong Kong's autonomy and democracy that was guaranteed by the Joint Declaration by Britain and China in 1984. Beijing has not hesitated to resort to the tactics of the Cultural Revolution in denouncing democracy advocates in the territory as "clowns" and "traitors."[203] Over the years, journalists, radio talk-show hosts and other voices of democracy in Hong Kong have been systematically harassed and intimidated with threats of violence and death-threats in an increasingly "suffocating" political atmosphere. Finally on April 26, 2004, Beijing came out openly and declared the barring of popular elections for Hong Kong's chief executive in 2007, and ruled out any expanded use of democratic voting for the legislature in 2008. Flatly rejecting complaints by the British and U.S. government, Beijing backed up its decision with the first military show of force since the territory's transfer to China by Britain in 1997. On May 5th this year, a flotilla of eight Chinese warships: two guided missile destroyers, four guided missiles frigates and two submarines sailed slowly down Victoria harbor, choosing the most visible route across the entire length of the harbor-front.[204]

Q. Wouldn't a boycott of Chinese products hurt the American economy? After all the economies of the two countries have now become so close and intertwined.

A. Yes, the American economy has become as dependent on import of Chinese products as it has on Saudi oil. And yes, if America were forced to give up either (or both) overnight — cold turkey — the national economy would certainly take a hit. But no one is advocating that. As with Saudi oil, it only makes sense to see that near exclusive dependence on import of Chinese products (no matter how cheap), is not a healthy habit, and that America should in both cases start looking for alternate sources for such products. And it further makes sense to ensure that such sources should, as far as possible, not originate from, and not financially benefit, countries that are openly or furtively working to undermine democracy and open society.

Q. There are labor abuses and other human rights violations in India, Mexico, Bangladesh and elsewhere. Why just pick on China?

A. Well, there are human rights violations right here in the United States too, but we are not calling for Americans to boycott their own products. In the end, it probably comes down to a question of degree, and China's human rights record is certainly an extreme one. No country in the world could be indicted with such a wide variety of horrendous and bizarre human rights abuses as China — as this book catalogues.

A useful starting-point for deciding on a particular boycott is to ask if the nation in question is a democracy or not. Mexico, Bangladesh, the Philippines and Indonesia all have human rights problems. Yet, these are also countries that have made the conscious and difficult choice to become democracies. They no doubt face enormous problems and even setbacks from time to time, but as long as they keep moving, even stumbling unsteadily, towards the goal of democracy, that is all we can ask of them at the moment. Strengthening the economy of such nations through trade could only benefit the cause of democracy worldwide. This in turn can only benefit free trade, as rule-of-law, transparency-in-government, empowered labor and a free media are probably the only ways through which a level economic playing-field can eventually be created for everyone.

Q. But insisting that China observe Western concepts of democracy and human rights might be regarded as cultural arrogance. After all the Chinese have their own Confucian value system where individual freedom is not so important as hierarchy and obedience.

A. Actually the sage is on record as saying, "Let humanity be your highest standard." Confucius may not exactly have been a democrat by present-day standards but he believed in the rule of law and accountability in government. Though he believed in the necessity of hierarchy and ritual in the running of a kingdom, he also absolutely believed that princes should rule through moral authority and not by violence and oppression. An even more humanist and democratic side of Confucianism is represented in the teachings of Mencius who not only put the interests of the people above that of the ruler but even vindicated tyrannicide.

At the end of the 19th century, the neo-Confucian scholar Kang Yu Wei (1858-1927), China's first great modern reformer, came up with a radical interpretation of Confucius' teaching which shook the intellectual world of the Chinese gentry-literati. In Kang's view, Confucius was a forward looking "sage king" who saw history as a progressive unilinear development from an age of disorder where kings and emperors ruled over people, to an age of universal peace and democratic government.

Long before the seeds of Communism were first planted in China, there was a broad intellectual movement towards democracy. "Mr. Democracy and Mr. Science" represented, for the youth and intelligentsia at the turn of the century (19th to 20th) in China, the two fundamental requisites for a modern Chinese state. The founding father of the modern Chinese state, Dr. Sun Yatsen, was a democrat. His widow, Song Meiling, together with Dr. Cai Yuanpei, chancellor of Beijing National University, and the writer, Lu Xun, founded the Chinese League for the Protection of Human Rights, as early as 1930.

It cannot be overly stressed that democracy and human rights do not just represent foreign values now being forced on a reluctant Chinese society. They existed in China's political debate since the end of the 19th century, appearing never to have existed only because of the effectiveness of totalitarian propaganda in blurring the political memory of an entire nation.

The notion of a set of "Asian Values" (as Confucian values are referred to in a larger context) of hierarchy, order and tradition that places little value on freedom and democracy can be dismissed outright if we take into account a very large portion of Asia that is oddly, but invariably, overlooked in this debate, the world's largest, and arguably liveliest democracy — India.

In his book, *Freedom As Development*, the Nobel Prize winning economist, Amartya Sen, delivers a withering critique of "Confucian values" and "Asian values." He holds up the examples of the Buddha, the Emperor Ashoka and the Moghul Emperor Akbar to demonstrate that such "Western values" as tolerance and freedom prevailed in Asia, on occasions even before they did in the West. Sen concludes, "To see Asian history in terms of a narrow category of authoritarian values does little justice to the rich varieties of thought in Asian intellectual tradition. Dubious history does nothing to vindicate dubious politics."[205]

Q. All the stores are flooded with "Made in China" products. How do we even begin to launch a boycott campaign?

A. It is precisely because there are so many Chinese products on the market that there is an opportunity to draw people's attention to this as a problem. The Burmese boycott faced the opposite predicament. There were so few "Made in Burma" products in Western stores that it was difficult to get people to even see the problem, much less become indignant about it. The overwhelming preponderance of "Made in China" products on store shelves nationwide demonstrate the hard fact that China is taking manufacturing jobs not only from developed countries, but even from Mexico, India, and Bangladesh — democracies where labor has certain rights. Even in poor, corrupt Cambodia, where the United Nations has managed to introduce a measure of democracy, including labor unions, and where in the last few years some international companies have set up some manufacturing units, especially in textiles and garments, jobs are now being lost to China. There is real fear among clothing manufacturers in Phnom Penh that in 2005 they could lose out to untrammeled competition from China. Although productions costs in Cambodia are far lower than most places in the world, they are nonetheless about 25 percent higher than in China, one reason being that Cambodian workers have union representation.[206]

A backlash against China's predatory export manufacturing started some years ago. South Korea's economic and finance minister, Jin Nyum, lamented at the end of 2001 that China was "turning itself into the world's manufacturing plant, which will suck all manufacturing facilities into it like a black hole." Newspapers from Japan to Singapore fretted that the Chinese export economy was "hollowing out" local manufacturing bases. The danger of China's export preponderance was clearly pointed out in the June 17, 2002 issue of *US Business Week,* in the article "When Everything Is Made In China," written by Jeffrey E. Garten, dean of the Yale School of Management. The article was vociferously condemned in major Chinese newspapers and journals.

From the beginning of 2004, we have had Lou Dobbs, the leading economic and financial expert for *CNN*, venting, on a near daily basis, on the loss of jobs and industries to China and other countries. Now with the U.S. presidential elections coming up at the end of this year, the major campaign issue dominating campaign debates and media discussions these days is the "outsourcing" of American jobs and industries.

Q. But Chinese products are so cheap...?

A. So is beef from cattle that has been fed the rendered bone, offal and blood of other slaughtered cattle. The chances of your being infected with CJD (the strain of Mad Cow disease that infects humans) from eating such beef may be absolutely remote, as state agricultural experts assure us, but the chances of your losing your job because of the proliferation of "Made in China" products is unquestionably more immediate. It should perhaps be emphasized that this analogy with Mad Cow Disease has not been made facetiously. Even from a moral point of view there is an unacceptable cannibal-like aspect to the buying of cheap "Made in China" products at the expense of the misery, suffering and even death of Chinese dissidents, *laogai* inmates and disenfranchised labor. Furthermore, who is to gainsay that the inroad of such products has not already begun to infect the economic and political system of the free world with a strain of China's congenital despotism?

Q. The Chinese economy is so huge and apparently booming. How can we expect to make even the tiniest impression on it with our boycott?

A. In spite of the impressive PR job by China and its supporters, it is not exactly a secret that the Chinese economy is facing tremendous problems. Much of this has been discussed in the chapter, "China Does Not Play By the Usual Rules of Business." In addition to the references cited in that chapter, Gordon G. Chang's, *The Coming Collapse of China*, must be mentioned. It is a compelling account of the rot in China's institutions and the forces at work that could bring about the end of the present People's Republic.

What Enron and WorldCom should have painfully taught everyone in the USA is that the volume of hype about an investment is usually in direct proportion to the chances of that venture being a scam. In the history of commerce, there has been no greater hype than that generated by the China trade.

While on the subject of economic bubbles and collapsing systems it might be noted that that on June 4, 2004, the *BBC* reported on the growing scale of protests and demonstrations in China, "The Ministry of Public Security says last year there were more than 58,000 "mass incidents" — the term they use to describe public protests — involving three million people: that is an increase of almost 15 percent over the year before." The figures also confirmed police sources that the protests were growing in size and number and becoming better organized. The report mentions that the protesters were largely peasants and workers. "One Western academic has warned that, when it comes to the growing unrest, China's leaders will face riskier dilemmas than at any time since the massive protests in 1989."[207]

That the end of days for China's Communist dynasty is rapidly approaching is spelled out in no uncertain terms by veteran China correspondent, Bruce Gilley, in his recent book.[208] Yet, convincing as Gilley's information and arguments that the regime will probably collapse before 2020, less convincing is his hope that the transition will be one to a democracy. This will happen, according to Gilley, not by popular overthrow of the regime but through gradual reforms from above, for China's elite will by then have become more public-spirited and less self-interested. Such faith in a moral elite (a/k/a reformists, pragmatists, modernists) has been the hallmark of China apologists, but recent trends in Chinese political culture point toward deepening corruption and cynicism rather than such a moral revival.

Q. I've visited Beijing and Shanghai, and frankly I didn't witness the abuses listed in the book.

A. You could have visited Nazi Germany in the mid-1930s and you wouldn't have seen the concentration camps and the persecution of Jews either, but it was happening all the same. What you would have seen would have been a dynamic Germany, where workers were (unlike in present-day China) getting decent wages, state healthcare, and even government subsidized holidays. Of course labor leaders were being imprisoned and executed, but as in China you wouldn't have seen it. Your eyes would instead have been dazzled by such great public projects as the world's first network of superhighways, the Autobahn, and to put the population on wheels, the "People's Car," the Volkswagon, so compact and inexpensive that the average German could afford it.

Your visit to Nazi Germany would have been, environmentally speaking, a far more pleasant experience than your China trip. In line with his personal obsession with cleanliness, the problem of pollution so concerned Hitler that he encouraged industry to work toward the complete elimination of noxious gases. Anti-pollution contrivances were already installed in some factories in the Ruhr basin, and new plants were required to construct preventive devices to avoid pollution of the waters.[209] And, of course, the Berlin Olympics of 1936 was a tremendous showcase for Nazi Germany as the Beijing Olympics will most certainly be for Communist/Fascist China in 2008.

The Russian poet Osip Mandelstam said, in sad amazement, that people thought life was normal because the streetcars were running. Not only were the streetcars running during Stalin's "Great Terror", but Moscow's great subway system was being built.

Q. But we're doing everything we can already: demonstrations, protests, letter-writing campaigns. You name it we're doing it. Why should a boycott be more effective?

A. So far, much of Tibetan activism against China has been either symbolic (Tenth March parades, demonstrations, freedom concerts, peace marches, even the Beijing Olympic protest) or supplicatory (signature drives, petitions, letter-writing campaigns). Such actions have definitely been useful, drawing public attention to the Tibetan cause and sometimes even embarrassing China.

But it is imperative that we seek a course of action that not only causes direct tangible injury, loss or disadvantage to China, but one that is also unequivocally non-violent, in a dynamic Gandhian way. Right at the moment China is most sensitive to economic loss. Without being in the least bit cynical, one could assert that depriving China of trade dollars would make a more forceful and deeply felt impact on Beijing than, say for instance, causing the death of some of its citizens through violence. The Chinese leadership is doing a pretty good job of that, in any case.

Q. But all governments in Europe, the US and Asia want to do business with China. What can we do without the support of these governments?

A. It is precisely because of this problem that a broad, people-oriented campaign like ours can succeed. Aung San Suu Kyi said, "Sometimes it is better to have the people of the world on your side than the governments of the world." As has been stated earlier, the nonviolent but morally powerful method we have chosen will, because of its grass-roots nature, take some time to deliver results. Yet, this drawback is more than compensated for by the fact that it is a strategy that does not depend for its success on the goodwill or intercession of politicians, bankers or businessmen — people who are most susceptible to China's economic blandishments. Nevertheless, as the campaign gains public support and media attention, politicians will jump on the bandwagon. They wouldn't be politicians if they didn't.

Q. We've done boycotts and "Toycotts" before and they didn't work. Why should the boycott work now?

A. The boycotts organized by the US Tibet Committee and the Canada Tibet Committee did work. In fact, they worked much better than expected. These campaigns did not fail but were stopped because the Tibetan government-in-exile hoped that by adopting a policy of "constructive engagement" with China, Beijing would agree to negotiations. This has, not surprisingly, failed to happen. The Milarepa Foundation also started a boycott campaign but withdrew when it was criticized for hurting the livelihood of ordinary Chinese people and of "China bashing."

Q. Well, isn't the boycott going to hurt the Chinese people? Isn't it, in fact, "China bashing?"

A. China bashing, or rather "Chinese bashing" is what the Communist Party leadership in Beijing did when it ordered T-69 tanks to roll over the bodies of thousands of peaceful Chinese demonstrators. "China bashing" is what State Security personnel are doing right now — beating and torturing peaceful worshippers, democracy activists, and women who want to protect their unborn babies. What our campaign is doing is "China Aiding." This is, first and foremost, refusing to participate in the enrichment of Communist Party leaders and cadres (who directly or through a variety of proxies) own over 95 percent of China's economy, and the ruthless and unashamed exploitation of Chinese prisoners, workers and farmers. "China Aiding" is furthermore showing genuine concern for the fate of wretched Chinese prisoners suffering in forced labor camps, and expressing solidarity with Chinese workers and farmers struggling for their rights against a brutal and inhuman dictatorship.

Q. Isn't it a fact that most "Made in China" products are bought by working-class people or minorities like Blacks and Hispanics, the kind of people who are least interested in Tibet or human rights issues?

A. That is elitist talk. Of course, it is only sensible to introduce the campaign to such people (or anyone else for that matter) on a note that is familiar or important to that person or group. For instance, with Blacks it may be a good idea to discuss

Archbishop Desmond Tutu's or Nelson Mandela's views on economic boycotts. With Hispanics and Latinos, one could, perhaps, start the discussion with accounts of the persecution of Catholics in China and the plight of Chinese bishops in forced labor camps. In rural America, one could publicize the plight of Protestant pastors and churches persecuted by China's state security, and also the issue of "forced abortions." Of course, it can be further argued that such sections of American society suffer most from inroads of Chinese goods, when industry declines in this country and decent-paying manufacturing jobs grow fewer every day.

There is a charming photograph from Gandhi's visit to England in 1931. Wrapped in a woolen shawl and looking happy but somewhat bashful, he is surrounded by tough-looking but friendly female mill workers in Lancashire who are giving him a rousing welcome. These were people driven to unemployment by Gandhi's boycott of British textiles. Yet, they are cheering the Mahatma and raising their fists in the air in solidarity with him. It is outrageously condescending, to say the least, for privileged people to assume that the working class will not respond to overtures about human rights and freedom, but only their self-interests.

Q. Could we tie-in the "Made in China" boycott with the boycott of French wines and products that seems to have started in the USA?

A. Thane Peterson, columnist for *Business Week*, rightly maintains that "boycotting French and German products is silly. If Americans really want to make a political statement at the mall, try avoiding Chinese goods." He elaborates on the issue: "Targeting France and Germany is also anti-democratic. The establishment of a strong democracy in Germany is one of the greatest accomplishments of the post-World War II era...

American soldiers didn't fight and die in World War II to establish lapdog governments in Europe. The goal was to promote freedom and democracy — which, whether you agree with their specific policies or not, is what we now have in France and Germany."

"China, however, is another kettle of fish. It's ruled by a cabal of aging, unelected autocrats. It jails or deports dissidents who agitate for democracy or openly believe in religions deemed unacceptable to the government, such as Falun Gong. It's trying to crush Tibet, a peaceful Buddhist nation, and would dearly like to take control of Taiwan, a long-time American ally. It employs prison labor and forces abortions on many of its own citizens. To my mind, China also represents a major economic threat to the U.S."[210]

However, in the light of recent reports of the French conducting joint naval exercises with the Chinese navy, and even otherwise cozying up with Beijing in general, it is perhaps, not morally incumbent on us to make too great an effort at dissuading those calling for a boycott of French products.

Q. Isn't it more practical to focus on "specific targets" like the World Bank or a corporation doing business with China than undertake a broad boycott?

A. In any discussion on boycotts there is a good deal of resistance to a boycott that is not targeted at specific companies. The logic being that targeting a specific company is more realistic and more immediately achievable than a broad campaign. But is it? A longtime American observer of the Tibetan scene put it very succinctly in a discussion:

"People keep saying that they loved the Holiday Inn campaign. But what kind of victory was that? What goal did it serve other than to remove a hotel from Lhasa? To what extent did it do anything to cause the Chinese to reverse their oppressive policies in Tibet? All it did was allow those on the outside to pat themselves on the back for a job well done."

In the military, it is axiomatic that "special operations" are only useful within the context of a broader campaign. One is not saying here that Support Groups should not target specific companies or financial institutions doing business with China, but that such specific operations only have meaning and will benefit the cause if there is a broader economic campaign to which it can contribute. Otherwise, such target-specific projects, by themselves, serve only as symbolic gestures.

Targeting individual companies to resolve the Tibetan issue is a bit like attempting to empty an ocean with a spoon. The boycott campaign on the other hand is not about defeating companies or corporations one by one. It is rather about creating a "chain-reaction" of moral outrage among consumers all over the world against China's crimes.

Q. After 9/11 and the Iraq War, nobody's interested in China's human rights violations or Tibetan freedom. If you had a terrorist angle to tie in with your boycott campaign maybe you might get a response. Could you think up one?

A. There is no need to make up or invent anything here. Just read the chapter on "World's Largest Supplier of Nuclear Weapons to Rogue States" in this book. There is every reason and more to boycott "Made in China" on just this one issue.

Q. But I am already involved in major campaigns for the Tibetan cause. Is it really necessary for me to participate in one more action as this?

A. Anyone involved in the Tibetan struggle, in any way, must absolutely undertake a personal boycott of Chinese products. Every time we buy a "Made in China" product we are doing business with China. For an activist to permit this in his daily life, while loudly denouncing American banks or multinational corporations for doing business with China would be the ultimate hypocrisy.

Notes

[1] Al Franken, *Lies and the Lying Liars Who Tell Them: A Fair and Balanced Look at the Right*, Dutton, New York, 2003.

[2] Ibid.

[3] Paul Krugman, "The China Syndrome", *The New York Times*, May 13, 2003.

[4] Robert Kagan, "Why Democracy Must Remain America's Goal Abroad: The Ungreat Washed" (A review of Fareed Zakaria's *The Future of Freedom*), *The New Republic Online*, July 7, 2003.

[5] Jane Kramer, "All He Surveys: Silvio Berlusconi liked Italy so much he Bought the Country", *The New Yorker*, November 10, 2003.

[6] Joe Studwell, *The China Dream: The Quest for the Last Great Untapped Market on Earth*, Atlantic Monthly Press, New York, 2002, pp. 119-121.

[7] James Mann, *About Face: A History of America's Curious Relationship with China, From Nixon to Clinton*, Knopf, New York, 1999, p. 287.

[8] Perry Link, "The Anaconda in the Chandelier", *The New York Review of Books*, April 11, 2002.

[9] Laurie Goodstein, "For Harmony, Dalai Lama Stays Home: U.N. Peace Meeting Tried to Please China", *The New York Times*, August 3, 2000.

[10] Elliot Sperling, "The Rhetoric of Dissent", in *Resistance and Reform in Tibet*, Robert Barnett & Shirin Akiner (eds.), Hurst, London, 1994.

[11] Hongda Harry Wu, *Laogai: The Chinese Gulag*, Westview, Boulder, 1992, p. 49.

[12] Ed Bradley, *Made in China*, 60 Minutes, CBS, September 15, 1991.

[13] Bao Ruo Wang, *Prisoner of Mao*, Coward, McCann, Geoghegan, New York, 1973.

[14] Abraham Verghese, "Changing Hearts", *The New York Times Magazine*, March 10, 2002.

[15] Erik Eckholm, "Mine Flood Shows How China Uses Prison Labor", *The New York Times*, May 22, 2001.

[16] William K. Rashbaum, "Clip Manufacturer in China Convicted of Forced Labor", *The New York Times*, March 1, 2001.

[17] Philip P. Pan, "China's Prison Laborers Pay Price for Market Reforms", *Washington Post Foreign Service*, June 14, 2001.

[18] Ibid

[19] Ibid.

[20] Harry Wu, *Troublemaker: One Man's Crusade Against China's Cruelty*, Times Books, New York, 1996.

[21] Richard Bernstein & Ross H. Munro, *The Coming Conflict With China*, Knopf, New York, 1997, p.130.

[22] David Phinny, "Toys for Tots and Profits", ABCNews.com, Special Report, http://abcnews.go.com/sections/world/hongkong97/pla_companies.html

[23] Kenneth de Graffenreid (ed.), *The Cox Report: The Unanimous and Bipartisan Report of the House Select Committee on U.S. National Security and Military Commercial Concerns with the People's Republic of China*, Regenry, Washington, D.C., 1999.

[24] Johanna McGeary, "The Next Cold War", *Time Magazine*, June 7, 1999.

[25] Edward Timperlake & William C. Triplett II, *Year of the Rat: How Bill Clinton Compromised U.S. Security for Chinese Cash*, Regnery, Washington, D.C., 1998.

[26] Stephen Labaton, "Advisor to U.S. Aided Maker of Satellites", *The New York Times*, March 29, 2003.

[27] David Shambaugh, *Modernizing China's Military: Progress, Problems, and Prospects*, University of California Press, Berkeley, 2002, pp. 188-89.

[28] "China's Military Fires Daily Blast at Taiwan, Needle at USA", Taiwan Security Research, *Agence France Presse*, March 7, 2000.

[29] David Shambaugh, *Modernizing China's Military*. p. 304.

[30] Ross H. Munro, "Eavesdropping on the Chinese Military: Where it Expects War –Where it Doesn't", *Orbis*, Summer 1994.

[31] Anthony Faiola, "China Claims Ancient Kingdom; Koreas Believe Neighbor is Trying to Use Dynasty as Border Battle Fodder", *Washington Post*, January 26, 2004.

[32] Sandeeep Unnithan, "Ship Shape," *India Today International*, May 12, 2003.

[33] "China and India accuse each other of cross-border intrusion," *AFP*, Beijing, July 25, 2003.

[34] David Shambaugh, *Modernizing China's Military*. pp. 306-307.

[35] Willy Wo-Lap Lam, "China Readies for Future U.S. Fight", March 25, 2003. *CNN.com/WORLD*, http://www.cnn.com/2003/WORLD/asiapcf/east/03/24/willy.column/

[36] Willy Wo-Lap Lam, "Why War is Reviving Spirit of Mao", *CNN.com/World* April 1, 2003, http://edition.cnn.com/2003/WORLD/asiapcf/east/03/31/willy.column/

[37] Thom Shanker, "U.S. Says China Is Stepping Up Short-Range Missile Production", *The New York Times*, July 31, 2003.

[38] John Pomfret "China Warns Taiwan That Attack May Be 'Unavoidable", *Washington Post Foreign Service*, November 20, 2003.

[39] Joseph Kahn, "Chinese Officers Say Taiwan Leaders Are Near 'Abyss of War'", *The New York Times*, December 4, 2003.

[40] Han Dongfang, "A Long Hard Journey: The Rise of a Free Labor Movement", *China Rights Forum*, Winter 1995. http://gb.hrichina.org/gate/gb/iso.hrichina.org:8151/old_site/crf/english/95winter/e9.html?

[41] Joseph Kahn, "When Chinese Workers Unite, The Bosses Often Run the Union", *The New York Times*, December 29, 2003.

[42] "China Has Jailed Many Labor Activists", *Labor Rights Now*, a UAW and A.F.L.-C.I.O. joint project, http://www.uaw.org/action/china/free03.html

[43] "Report of the Working Group on Enforced or Involuntary Disappearances," E/CN.4/1995/36 (excerpt) [p.64], Commission on Human Rights, United Nations, December 30, 1994.

[44] Han Dongfang, "A Long Hard Journey."

[45] Jasper Becker, *The Chinese*, Free Press, Simon and Schuster, New York, 2000.

[46] *The China Labor Bulletin*, No. 57, November - December 2000, http://www.china-labour.org.hk/iso/

[47] Anita Chan, *China's Workers Under Assault: The Exploitation of Labor in a Globalizing Economy*, M.E Sharpe, New York, 2001.

[48] "How Wal-Mart is Remaking our World," *The Hightower Lowdown*, Vol. 4, No. 4, April 2002.

[49] *Wal-Mart Dungeon in China, Qin Shi Handbag Factory*, National Labor Committee, http://www.nlcnet.org/campaigns/archive/chinareport/walmart.shtml

[50] *Toys of Misery 2004, A Joint Report by National Labor Committee and China Labor Watch*, National Labor Committee, February 2004, http://www.nlcnet.org/campaigns/he-yi/he-yi.shtml

[51] Jasper Becker, "China's Exploited Toy Workers Still Toil in Toxic Sweatshops", *The Independent*, December 24, 2002.

[52] Peter S. Goodman and Philip P. Pan, "Chinese Workers Pay for Wal-Mart's Low Prices; Retailer Squeezes Its Asian Suppliers to Cut Costs", *Washington Post Foreign Service*, February 8, 2004.

[53] Joseph Kahn, "China's Workers Risk Limbs in Export Drive", *The New York Times*, April 7, 2003.

[54] "Chinese Underground", *The New York Times Magazine*, July 13, 2003.

[55] Erick Eckholm, "Tide of China's Migrants: Flowing to Boom, or Bust?", *The New York Times*, July 29, 2003.

[56] Bruce Gilley, "Toil and Trouble: Slavery is on the Rise in China as the Number of Poor Migrants Increases", *Far Eastern Economic Review*, August 16, 2001.

[57] "Funing Police Put Labor Activist in Mental Hospital Under False Pretenses", *China Labor Watch*, December 15, 2000, http://www.chinalaborwatch.org/index.htm, http://www.chinalaborwatch.org/releases/001215cao-hospital.htm

[58] Philip P. Pan, "High Tide of Labor Unrest in China", *Washington Post Foreign Service*, January 21, 2002.

[59] Joseph Kahn, "Chinese Girls' Toil Brings Pain, Not Riches", *The New York Times*, October 2, 2003.

[60] Stephen Greenhouse and Elizabeth Becker, "A.F.L.-C.I.O. To Press Bush For Penalties Against China", *The New York Times*, March 16, 2004.

[61] Willy Wo-Lap Lam, "Beijing Faces Winter of Discontent", September 30, 2003, *CNN.com/World*, http://edition.cnn.com/2003/WORLD/asiapcf/east/09/29/willy.column/index.html

[62] Joseph Kahn, "Exposé of Peasants' Plight is Suppressed by China," *The New York Times*, July 9, 2004.

[63] Human Rights Watch/Asia, *State Control of Religion, Update No. 1*, March 1998. Earlier publications on the subject by Human Rights Watch include *Freedom of Religion in China*, 1992, *Continuing Religious Repression in China*, 1993, and *Religious Persecution Persists*, 1995.

[64] *Report Analyzing Seven Secret Chinese Government Documents*, Center For Religious Freedom, Freedom House, Washington, D.C., February 11, 2002.

[65] Joseph Kahn, "U.S. Panel on Religious Freedom Drops China Visit, Protesting Curbs", *The New York Times*, August 8, 2003.

[66] *Dangerous Meditation: China's Campaign Against Falungong*, Human Rights Watch, New York, January 2002.

[67] Ibid.

[68] Maria Hsia Chang, *Falun Gong: The End of Days*, Yale University Press, New Haven, 2004.

[69] Tibet Information Network (TIN) News Update / 19 August 2001; *Destruction of Serthar Institute : A Special Report*, Tibetan Centre for Human Rights & Democracy, 2002.

[70] See http://www.tchrd.org/pubs/serthar/

[71] Tibet Information Network (TIN) News Update / 27 January 2003.

[72] Erik Eckholm, "From a Chinese Cell, A Lama's Influence Remains Undimmed", *The New York Times*, February 23, 2003.

[73] Philip P. Pan, "In the Name of the Panchen Lama Tibetans Cling to Icon as China Restricts Religious, Cultural Freedom", *Washington Post Foreign Service*, September 19, 2003.

[74] "Prisoners of Religious Conscience for the Underground Roman Catholic Church in China", Cardinal Kung Foundation, updated July 19, 2003, http://cardinalkungfoundation.org/prisoners/index.html

[75] "Hong Kong: Bishop Criticizes China," *New York Times*, February 18, 2003.

[76] China Tightening Its Grip on Catholics", *Zenit* News Agency, Rome, May 28, 2003.

[77] "Vatican Condemns Chinese Arrests", *BBC News*, 2004/06/23 16:38:08 GMT, http://news.bbc.co.uk/go/pr/fr/-/2/hi/asia-pacific/3833861.stm

[78] Craig S. Smith, "2 Christians Ordered to Die as China Acts Against a Sect", *The New York Times*, December 31, 2001.

[79] Erik Eckholm, "3 Church Leaders in China Are Sent to Prison for Life", *The New York Times*, October 11, 2002.

[80] "China Sentences Man on Reduced Charge for Importing Bibles", *The New York Times*, January 29, 2002.

[81] *Persecution of a Protestant Sect*, Human Rights Watch, New York, Vol. 6, No. 6, June 1994.

[82] *1990 Population Census of China*, State Statistical Bureau, Beijing, 1992.

[83] Dr. Paul George, "Islamic Unrest in the Xinjiang Uighur Autonomous Region," *Commentary*, No. 73, A Canadian Security Intelligence Service Publication, Spring 1998.

[84] Ibid.

[85] "UAA Testifies in U.S. Senate", Uyghur Information Agency, Washington, D.C., August 8, 2002.

[86] Dr. Paul George, "Islamic Unrest in the Xinjiang Uighur Autonomous Region".

[87] Erkin Dolat, "The U.S. Has Justified Chinese Persecution of the Uyghur People", Uyghur Information Agency, Washington, D.C., August 27, 2002.

[88] Jim Yardley, "China Brands Muslim Groups As Terrorists", *The New York Times*, December 16, 2003.

[89] Steven W. Mosher, "A Mother's Ordeal", *Reader's Digest*, February, 1987, pp. 49-55.

[90] Statement of Gao Xiao Duan. Planned-birth officer. "Forced Abortion and Sterilization in China : The View From the Inside." Hearing before the Subcommittee on International Operations and Human Rights of the Committee on International Relations, One Hundred Fifth Congress, Second Session, June 10, 1998 (SuDoc Y 4.IN 8/16:AB 7).

[91] J.S. Aird, *Slaughter of the Innocents: Coercive Birth Control in China*, AEI Press, Washington D.C., 1990.

[92] Statement of Gao Xiao Duan. Planned-birth officer.

[93] Statement of Zhou Shiu Yon, victim of China's planned-birth-policy. "Forced abortion and Sterilization in China : The View from the Inside." Hearing Before the Subcommittee on International Operations and Human Rights of the Committee on International Relations, One Hundred Fifth Congress, Second Session, June 10, 1998 (SuDoc Y 4.IN 8/16:AB 7).

[94] Quotations taken from: "China's Coercive Birth Control Programme," Independent Tibet Network UK, London, http://www.tibettruth.com/birthcontrolprog.html

[95] Steven Mufson, *Washington Post*, December 22, 1993.

[96] Quotations taken from: "China's Coercive Birth Control Programme," Independent Tibet Network UK, London, http://www.tibettruth.com/birthcontrolprog.html

[97] Martin Moss & Jeffrey Bowe, *Orders of the State: Responsibility and Collaboration in China's Population Programme*, Independent Tibet Network UK, 2000.
Independent Tibet Network, *Children of Despair: An Analysis of Coercive Birth Control in Chinese Occupied Tibet*, ITN, UK, 1992.
Tibetan Women's Association, *Tears of Silence: A Report on Tibetan Women and Population Control*. TWA, Dharamshala, India, 1995.

[98] John Gittings, "Claims of Forced Abortions in Tibet are Untrue, says report," *The Guardian*, February 25, 2002.

[99] "Men Without Women: The Consequence of Family Planning", *The Economist*, June 22, 2002.

[100] Elisabeth Rosenthal, "Bias for Boys Leads to Sale of Baby Girls in China", *The New York Times*, July 20, 2003.

[101] Jasper Becker, *The Chinese*, The Free Press, New York, 2000.

[102] "Relying on Hard and Soft Sells, India Pushes Sterilization", *The New York Times*, Friday, June 22, 2001.
"Population Estimates Fall as Poor Women Assert Control," *The New York Times*, March 10, 2002.

[103] *China: The Death Penalty in 1999*, Amnesty International, February 2001, AI Index: ASA 17/005/2001.

[104] *People's Republic of China: Death Penalty Log, 1999*, Amnesty International, 2000, AI Index: ASA 17/49/00.

[105] "China Dramatically Increases Executions", *Death Penalty News*, Amnesty International, London, September 2001.

[106] Mike Melnyk, "From a Tourist, Travelling and Teaching in China and Tibet - May 2001", http://www.geocities.com/rusft/read-0105.html

[107] "China Dramatically Increases Executions", *Death Penalty News*, Amnesty International, London, September 2001.

[108] Craig S. Smith, "In Shift, Chinese Carry Out Executions by Lethal Injection", *The New York Times*, December 28, 2001.

[109] Ibid.

[110] "Mobile Vans Use Lethal Injection to Kill Chinese Prisoners", *Death Penalty News*, Amnesty International, London, March 2003.

[111] "China: Threat of Death Penalty for Breaches of SARS Regulation", Amnesty International, London, May 23, 2003, AI Index: ASA 17/024/2003.

[112] "Organ Procurement and Judicial Execution in China," Human Rights Watch/Asia, New York, Vol. 6, No. 9, August 1994.

[113] Craig S. Smith, "On Death Row, China's Source of Transplant", *The New York Times*, October 18, 2001.

[114] Ibid.

[115] Benjamin Weiser, "Absent Witness Spurs Judge to Delay Trial of 2 in Organ Sales Plan", *The New York Times*, March 2, 1999. "The International Sale of Chinese Prisoners' Organs: Who is the Real Criminal?", Laogai Research Foundation, http://www.laogai.org/news/organs/criminal.htm

[116] "Blood Money", *Prime Time Live* (News Magazine), ABC News, October 15, 1997.

[117] Thomas Fuller, "An Execution for a Kidney: China Supplies Convict's Organs to Malaysians", *International Herald Tribune*, June 15, 2000.

[118] Craig S. Smith, "Doctor Says He Took Transplant Organs From Executed Chinese Prisoners", *The New York Times*, June 29, 2001.

[119] Craig S. Smith "Quandary in U.S. Over Use of Organs of Chinese Inmates", *The New York Times*, November 11, 2001.

[120] Bill Kurtis, "The Organ Trade: Life and Death for Sale, Investigative Reports with Bill Kurtis, 9pm ET, August, 10, 1999, *A&E Network*, USA.

[121] "Black Market in Organs", In The Money, *CNN*, 2:30 pm CT, September 7, 2003.

[122] "Sell Yourself for Cash, Selling One's Own Body Parts", *MSNBC*, 7pm CT, January 18, 2004.

[123] *Peoples Republic of China, Torture and Ill-Treatment: Comment on China's Second Periodic Report to the UN Committee Against Torture*, Amnesty International, April 1996, AI Index: ASA 17/051/1996.

[124] *People's Republic of China: Torture – A Growing Scourge in China – Time for Action*, Amnesty International, February 2001, AI Index: ASA 17/004/2001.

[125] "Tales of Terror: Torture in Tibet (TCHRD)", *World Tibet News Network*, January 6, 1999.

[126] *A Generation in Peril: The Lives of Tibetan Children Under Chinese Rule*, International Committee of Lawyers for Tibet, San Francisco, March 2001.

[127] Craig S. Smith, "Torture Hurries New Wave of Executions in China', *The New York Times*, September 9, 2001.

[128] "Judicial Psychiatry in China and its Political Abuses", *Columbia Journal of Asian Law*, Vol. 14 No. 1, 2001.

[129] Robin Munro, *Dangerous Minds: Political Psychiatry in China Today and its Origins in the Mao Era*, Human Rights Watch/Geneva Initiative on Psychiatry, August 2002.

[130] Jonathan Mirsky, "China's Psychiatric Terror", *The New York Review of Books*, February 27, 2003.

[131] *Renmin Gongan Bao (People's Public Security News)*, May 18, 1990, p. 1.

[132] Erik Eckholm, "Psychiatrists Rebuke China For Blocking Inspection Visit", *The New York Times*, May 31, 2003.

[133] Melissa Harris & Sidney Jones (eds.), *Tibet Since 1950: Silence, Prison, or Exile*, Aperture/Human Rights Watch, New York, 2000.

[134] "Tibetans Will Soon be a Minority in Lhasa, Admits Official", *South China Morning Post*, August 8, 2002.

[135] Indira A.R. Lakshmanan, "Deemed a road to ruin, Tibetans say Beijing railway poses latest threat to minority culture", *Boston Globe*, August 26, 2002.

[136] Patrick French, *Tibet, Tibet: A Personal History of a Lost Land*, Harper Collins India, New Delhi, 2003, pp. 206-7.

[137] James Brooke, "Over Protests, Nepal Lets Chinese Force Refugees Back to Tibet", *The New York Times*, June 1, 2003.

[138] "Nepal Deports 18 Tibetans", *BBC NEWS*, May 31, 2003, http://news.bbc.co.uk/go/pt/fr/-/2/hi/south_asia/2952698.stm

[139] Linda Benson, *The Ili Rebellion: The Moslem Challenge to Chinese Authority in Xinjiang 1944-1949*, M.E. Sharpe, New York, 1990.

[140] "Xinjiang after September 11", *Human Rights News*, Human Rights Watch, New York, October 2001.

[141] *China: Human Rights Concerns in Xinjiang,* Human Rights Watch (backgrounder), October 2001.

[142] Cao Chang-ching, "Between the Abortion Knife and Nuclear Testing", Part IV of VII of "The Fight for East Turkestan, *Taipei Times,* October 14, 1999.

[143] Ibid.

[144] "China Tightens Internet Control", *Human Rights News,* Human Rights Watch, August 1, 2001, http://www.hrw.org/press/2001/08/china-0801.htm

[145] "State Control of the Internet in China: Appeal Cases", November 2002, Amnesty International, AI Index: ASA 17/046/2002.

[146] Elisabeth Rosenthal, "Four Chinese Given Long Prison Terms for Discussing Politics", *The New York Times,* May 30, 2003.

[147] Erick Eckholm, "A Father's Cranky Essays on Web Site Put Son in Jail in China", *The New York Times,* May 24, 2001.

[148] Robert Marquand "The 'mouse' that caused an uproar in China", *The Christian Science Monitor* (csmonitor.com), November 6, 2003, http://www.csmonitor.com/2003/1106/p01s04-woap.html

[149] Joseph Kahn, "China Has World's Tightest Internet Censorship, Study Finds, *The New York Times,* December 4, 2002.

[150] Jonathan Zittrain & Benjamin Edelman, "Emperical Analysis of Internet Filtering in China", Berkman Center for Internet & Society, Harvard Law School, March 20, 2003, http://cyber.law.harvard.edu/filtering/china

[151] "China Toughens Obstacles to Internet Searches", *The New York Times,* September 12, 2002.

[152] Jennifer E. Lee, "Guerrilla Warfare Waged With Code", *The New York Times* (Circuits), October 10, 2002.

[153] Howard W. French, "Despite Act of Leniency, China Has Its Eye on the Web", *The New York Times,* 27 June, 2004.

[154] Ibid.

[155] Louisa Lim, "China to Censor Text Messages", *BBC*, 2 July, 2004, 08:47 GMT 09:47 UK, http://news.bbc.co.uk/2/hi/asia-pacific/3859403.stm

[156] Newbold, Jill R., "Aiding the Enemy: Imposing Liability on U.S. Corporations for Selling China Internet Tools to Restrict Human Rights." *Journal of Law, Technology and Policy*, Vol. 2003, Fall, Issue 2, http://www.jltp.uiuc.edu/current_abstracts.html

[157] "The Acquisition of Technology Relating to Weapons of Mass Destruction and Advanced Conventional Munitions," CIA Report to Congress, Washington, D.C., June 1997.

[158] "Worldwide Maritime Challenges 1997," Office of Naval Intelligence, Washington, D.C., March 1997.

[159] Erick Eckholm, "China Rejects Allegations On Improving Iraqi Weapons", *The New York Times*, March 7, 2003.

[160] "A Period of Consequences", September 23, 1999, *International Information Programs*, U.S. Department of State, http://usinfo.state.gov/topical/pol/ terror/01121002.htm

[161] Tom Zeller, "Psssst…Can I Get A Bomb Trigger?" (case overviews compiled by Jordan Richie and Gary Milhollin of the Wisconsin Project on Nuclear Arms Control), *The New York Times*, September 15, 2002.

[162] Tim Weiner, "U.S. And China Helped Pakistan Build Its Bomb," *The New York Times*, June 1, 1998.

[163] Joseph Cirincione, Jon B. Wolfsthal & Miriam Rajkumar, *Deadly Arsenals: Tracking Weapons of Mass Destruction*, Carnegie Endowment for International Peace, Washington, D.C., 2002.

[164] "The Acquisition of Technology Relating to Weapons of Mass Destruction and Advanced Conventional Munitions, July-December 2000", CIA Report to Congress, September 7, 2001.

[165] Seymour M. Hersh, "The Cold Test: What the Administration Knew About Pakistan and the North Korean Nuclear Program", *The New Yorker*, January 27, 2003.

[166] David E. Sanger & James Dao, "U.S. Says Pakistan Gave Technology to North Korea," *The New York Times*, October 18, 2003.

[167] David E. Sanger, "U.S. Rebukes Pakistanis For Lab's Aid to Pyongyang", *The New York Times*, April 1, 2003.

[168] Bill Keller, "The Thinkable", *The New York Times Magazine*, May 4, 2003.

[169] David E. Sanger, "In North Korea and Pakistan, Deep Roots of Nuclear Barter", *The New York Times*, November 24, 2002. .

[170] Pakistan's nuclear arsenal and superior delivery system has in a real sense neutralized India's overwhelming advantage in conventional military terms that it enjoyed over Pakistan. There is also a perception that India in conventional military terms has been catching up with China. A study in a Chinese defense journal stressed "how much more advanced India's armed forces are than the PLA in virtually all categories of conventional weapons." David Shambaugh, *Modernizing China's Military*. p. 306.

[171] Howard W. French, "Taboo Against Nuclear Arms Is Being Challenged in Japan", *The New York Times*, June 9, 2002.

[172] Joseph Kahn, "As U.S. and North Korea Glower, China Pushes for Talks", *The New York Times*, July 16, 2003.
Joseph Kahn, "China Pushes North Korea and U.S. Talks" *The New York Times*, July 18, 2003.

[173] Elizabeth Becker and Edmund L. Andrews, "China's Currency is Emerging in U.S. as Business Issue", *The New York Times*, August 26, 2003.

[174] Joseph Kahn, "Korea Arms Talks Close With Plans for a New Round", *The New York Times*, August 30, 2003.

[175] Joseph Kahn, "Chinese Aide Says U.S. is Obstacle in Korean Talks", *The New York Times*, September 2, 2003.

[176] David E. Sanger & William J. Broad, "From Rogue Nuclear Programs, Web of Trails Leads to Pakistan; A History of Denials and Hidden Proliferation", *The New York Times*, January 4, 2004.
Patrick E. Tayler & David E. Sanger, "Pakistan Called Libyans' Source of Atom Design; Key to Weapons Design", *The New York Times*, January 6, 2004.

[177] Joby Warrick and Peter Slevin, "Libyan Arms Designs Traced Back to China," *Washington Post*, February 15, 2004; p. A01, http://www.washingtonpost.com/wp-dyn/articles/A42692-2004Feb14.html.

[178] Ibid.

[179] Tom Zeller, "Psssst...Can I Get A Bomb Trigger?".

[180] *Reuters*, "China Helping Iran, North Korea on Weapons – Panel", *The New York Times*, June 15, 2004.

[181] Wayne M. Morrison, "Major Chinese Trade Barriers", *China-U.S. Trade Issues*, updated March 14, 2002, CRS Issue Brief for Congress, Congressional Research Service, The Library of Congress, pp. 6-8.

[182] "A Guardian of Jobs or a Reverse Robin Hood", *The New York Times*, September 1, 2002.

[183] "Malden Mills Fails to Win Loan Guarantee", *The New York Times*, August 26, 2003.

[184] Chris Buckley, "Helped by Technology, Piracy of DVD's Runs Rampant in China", *The New York Times*, August 18, 2003.

[185] "The World's Greatest Fakes", *60 Minutes II*, CBSNews.com, January 28, 2004.

[186] Ibid.

[187] Steve Lohr, "Fast Gaining in Technology China Poses Trade Worries", *The New York Times*, January 13, 2004.

[188] James Mann, *Beijing Jeep: A Case Study of Western Business in China*, Westview Press, Boulder, CO; 1997, p. 54.

[189] Joe Studwell, *The China Dream.*

[190] Nicholas Lardy, "China's Worsening Debts", *Financial Times,* June 21, 2001.
Mark Clifford, "Are China's Banks Caught in a Quicksand," *Business Week,* November 25, 2002.
Mark Clifford, "Bankrupt Logic About China's Debts," *China Journal,* November 22, 2002.
Liu Binyan & Perry Link, "A Great Leap Backward?", *The New York Review of Books,* October 8, 1998.

[191] Keith Bradsher, "Credit Agencies Worry About Health of China's Banks", *The New York Times,* November 6, 2003.

[192] Keith Bradsher "Has Irrational Exuberance Hit China?", *The New York Times,* December 14, 2003.

[193] Keith Bradsher, "Is China the Next Bubble", *The New York Times,* January 18, 2004.

[194] "Soaring imports from China push U.S. trade deficit to new record", *Trade Picture,* Economic Policy Institute, February 13, 2004, http://www.epinet.org/content.cfm/webfeatures_econindicators_tradepict

[195] William Safire, "Gravy Trains Don't Run On Time: Good Riddance, Singapore Model," *The New York Times,* January 19, 1998.
William Safire, "The Misrule of Law: Singapore's Legal Racket", *The New York Times,* January 6, 1997.

[196] Susan Njanji, "Mugabe looks to China" *News.Com.AU,* December 3, 2003, http://www.news.com.au/common/story_page/0,4057,8051718%255E1702,00.html

[197] Gal Luft & Anne Korin, The Sino-Saudi Connection, *Commentary,* March 2004, www.commentarymagazine.com/Archive/DigitalArchive.aspx?panes=1&aid=11703028_1

[198] Joseph Kahn, "China's Congress of Crony Capitalists", *The New York Times,* November 19, 2002.

[199] Bao Tong, "Faking Reforms at the Communist Party Congress", *The New York Times*, November 23, 2002.

[200] Jasper Becker, "Mussolini Redux", *The New Republic Online*, June 23, 2003.

[201] Jasper Becker, *The Chinese*, Free Press, New York, 2000.

[202] Joseph Kahn, "At Chinese Congress, Little Debate But Lots of Picture-Taking", *The New York Times*, November 11, 2002.

[203] Keith Bradsher, "Hong Kong Protesters Say China is Trying to Stifle Democracy", *The New York Times*, April 2, 2004.

[204] Keith Bradsher, "Flotilla is Beijing's Message to an Unsettled Hong Kong," *The New York Times*, May 6, 2004.

[205] Amartya Sen, *Development As Freedom*, Anchor Books, New York, 1999, pp. 231-248.

[206] James Brooke, "A Year of Worry for Cambodia's Garment Makers," *The New York Times*, January 24, 2004.

[207] Louisa Lim, "China Protest on the Rise", *BBC NEWS*, June 8, 2004, 10:21:20 GMT, http://news.bbc.co.uk/go/pr/fr/-/2/hi/asia-pacific/3786541.stm

[208] Bruce Gilley, *China's Democratic Future: How It Will Happen and Where It Will Lead*, Columbia University Press, New York, 2004.

[209] John Toland, *Adolf Hitler*, Doubleday, New York, 1976, p. 403.

[210] Thane Peterson, "Consumers Strike a Blow for Democracy", *Business Week*, March 18, 2003.

Select Bibliography

Aird, J.S. (1990). *Slaughter of the Innocents: Coercive Birth Control in China.* Washington, D.C.: AEI Press.

Amnesty International. (March 2003). "Mobile Vans Use Lethal Injection to Kill Chinese Prisoners." *Death Penalty News.* London: Author.

_______. (November 2002). *State Control of the Internet in China: Appeal Cases.* AI I Index: ASA 17/046/2002.

_______. (September 2001). "China Dramatically Increases Executions." *Death Penalty News.* London: Author.

_______. (February 2001). *People's Republic of China: Torture – A Growing Scourge in China – Time for Action.* AI Index: ASA 17/004/2001.

_______. (February 2001). *China: The Death Penalty in 1999.* AI Index: ASA 17/005/2001.

Bao Ruo Wang. (1973). *Prisoner of Mao.* New York: Coward, McCann, Geoghegan.

Becker, Jasper. (December 24, 2002). "China's Exploited Toy Workers Still Toil in Toxic Sweatshops." *The Independent.*

_______. (2000). *The Chinese.* New York: The Free Press.

Benson, Linda. (1990). *The Ili Rebellion: The Moslem Challenge to Chinese Authority in Xinjiang 1944-1949.* New York: M.E. Sharpe.

Bernstein, Richard and Ross H. Munro. (1997). *The Coming Conflict with China.* New York: Knopf.

Cardinal Kung Foundation. (2000). *Prisoners of Religious Conscience for the Underground Roman Catholic Church in China.* Stamford, CT: Author.

Chan, Anita. (2001). *China's Workers Under Assault: The Exploitation of Labor in a Globalizing Economy.* New York: M.E. Sharpe.

Chang, Gordon. (2001). *The Coming Collapse of China.* New York: Random House.

Chang, Maria Hsia. (2004). *Falun Gong: The End of Days.* New Haven: Yale University Press.

Cirincione, Joseph, John B. Wolfsthal and Miriam Rajkumar. (2002). *Deadly Arsenals: Tracking Weapons of Mass Destruction.* Washington, D.C.: Carnegie Endowment for International Peace.

Central Intelligence Agency. (September 2001). "Report to Congress: The Acquisition of Technology Relating to Weapons of Mass Destruction and Advanced Conventional Munitions, July – December 2000.". Washington, D.C.: Author.

_______. (June 1997). "Report to Congress: The Acquisition of Technology Relating to Weapons of Mass Destruction and Advanced Conventional Munitions." Washington, D.C.: Author.

de Graffenreid, Kenneth, ed. (1999). *The Cox Report: The Unanimous and Bipartisan Report of the House Select Committee on U.S. National Security and Military Commercial Concerns with the People's Republic of China.* Washington, D.C.: Regenry.

George, Paul. (Spring 1998). "Islamic Unrest in the Xinjiang Uigher Autonomous Region". *Commentary,* No. 73, A Canadian Security Intelligence Service Publication.

Gilley, Bruce. (2004). *China's Democratic Future: How It Will Happen and Where It Will Lead.* New York, Columbia University Press.

Harris, Melissa and Sidney Jones (eds). (2000). *Tibet Since 1950: Silence, Prison or Exile.* New York: Aperture/Human Rights Watch.

Hilton, Isabel. (1999). *The Search for the Panchen Lama.* New York: W.W. Norton & Company.

Hearing before the Subcommittee on International Operations and Human Rights of the Committee on International Relations. (June 10, 1998). Statement of Gao Xiao Duan, Planned-Birth Officer. "Forced Abortion and Sterilization in China: The View from the Inside." Washington, D.C.: House of Representatives, One Hundred Fifth Congress, Second Session. (SuDoc Y 4.IN 8/16:AB 7)

Human Rights Watch. (February 2004). *Trials of a Tibetan Monk: The Case of Tenzin Delek.* New York: Author.

_______. (2002). *Dangerous Meditation, China's Campaign Against Falungong.* New York: Author.

_______. (August 2001). "*China Tightens Internet Control*". Human Rights News. New York: Author.

_______. (1999). *China: State Control of Religion.* New York: Author.

_______. (June 1994). *Persecution of a Protestant Sect.* New York: Author.

Independent Tibet Network (1992). *Children of Despair: An Analysis of Coercive Birth Control in Chinese Occupied Tibet.* London: Author.

International Campaign for Tibet. (2004). *A Season to Purge: Religious Repression in Tibet,* Washington, D.C.: Author.

International Commission of Jurists. (1960). *Tibet and the Chinese People's Republic: A Report to the International Commission of Jurists by its Legal Inquiry Committee on Tibet.* Geneva: Author.

_______. *The Question of Tibet and the Rule of Law.* (1959). Geneva: Author.

International Committee of Lawyers for Tibet. (2001). *A Generation in Peril: The Lives of Tibetan Children Under Chinese Rule.* San Francisco: Author.

Link, Perry. (April 11, 2002). "The Anaconda in the Chandelier". *The New York Review of Books.*

Mann, James. (1999). *About Face: A History of America's Curious Relationship with China, From Nixon to Clinton.* New York: Knopf.

_______. (1997). *Beijing Jeep: A Case Study of Western Business in China.* Boulder, CO: Westview Press.

Mosher, Steven W. (2000). *China Hegemon: China's Plan to Dominate Asia and the World.* San Francisco: Encounter Books.

_______. (1993). *A Mother's Ordeal: One Woman's Fight Against China's One-Child Policy.* San Francisco: Harperperennial.

Moss, Martin and Jeffrey Bowe. (2000). *Orders of the State: Responsibility and Collaboration in China's Population Programme.* London: Independent Tibet Network.

Munro, Robin. (August 2002). *Dangerous Minds: Political Psychiatry in China Today and its Origins in the Mao Era.* New York and Geneva: Human Rights Watch/Geneva Initiative on Psychiatry.

National Labor Committee. (2004). *Wal-Mart Dungeon in China, Qin Shi Handbag Factory.* New York: Author.

_______. and China Labor Watch (February 2004). *Toys of Misery 2004.* New York: Authors.

Norbu, Jamyang. (2000). *Rangzen Charter: The Case for Tibetan Independence.* New York: Rangzen Alliance.

Shambaugh, David. (2002). *Modernizing China's Military: Progress, Problems, and Prospects.* Berkeley: University of California Press.

Studwell, Joe. (2002). *The China Dream: the Quest for the Last Great Untapped Market on Earth.* New York: Atlantic Monthly Press.

Tibetan Centre for Human Rights & Democracy. (2002). *Destruction of Serthar Institute: A Special Report.* Dharamshala, India: Author.

Timperlake, Edward and William C. Triplett II. (1999). *Red Dragon Rising, Communist China's Military Threat to America.* Washington, D.C.: Regenry.

_______. (1998). *Year of the Rat: How Bill Clinton Compromised U.S. Security for Chinese Cash.* Washington, D.C.: Regenry.

Tyler, Christian. (2003). *Wild West China: The Taming of Xinjiang.* New York: John Murray.

Wu, Hongda Harry. *Laogai: The Chinese Gulag.* (1992). Boulder, CO: Westview Press.

_______. with George Vecesey. (1996). *Troublemaker: One Man's Crusade Against China's Cruelty.* New York: Times Books.

ACKNOWLEDGMENTS

As mentioned in the introduction, most of the facts presented in this book have been taken from the reports and publications of the Laogai Foundation, Human Rights Watch, Amnesty International, National Labor Committee, Freedom House, China Rights Forum, Human Rights in China, Cardinal Kung Foundation, Carnegie Endowment for World Peace, Tibetan Information Network, Tibetan Centre for Human Rights and Democracy, Independent Tibet Network, Uyghur Information Agency, Geneva Initiative on Psychiatry and other human rights, religious, labor, intelligence, governmental, educational, advocacy and research organizations, as well as individual experts and scholars. The dedicated research work of these organizations and individuals has not only provided the substance of this book, but very often has been the source of the news reports that are otherwise also extensively quoted in the book. A tremendous debt of gratitude is owed to all of them.

Many thanks are also owed to Dr. Lisa S. Keary who has been the primary editor and moral instigator of this book. Lisa has devoted tremendous time and energy in the fulfillment of this project, and also contributed substantially to the initial research. I must also thank Prof. Elliot Sperling and Lucas Myers' editorial contributions and invaluable suggestions, and also Dr. Warren Smith for information and guidance. Many thanks to Phuntsok Jordhen for taking time off from a busy schedule to work on the design and layout of this book.

Finally, I would like to thank Champa and Robert Weinrab, the Milarepa Foundation and others for financial support; and Sonam Wangdu, Lhadon Tethong, Alma David, Students for a Free Tibet, and the US-Tibet Committee for their assistance and support.

Index

P

Q

R

S

V

W

X

Y

Z

ABOUT THE AUTHOR

Jamyang Norbu is one of Tibet's foremost writers at work today. His novel, *The Mandala of Sherlock Holmes,* won the prestigious Crossword Book Award, India's equivalent of the Booker Prize, and has been published in over a dozen languages. He is also the author of *Warriors of Tibet* and *Performing Traditions of Tibet.* The latter reflects his work as an ethnomusicologist and director of the Tibetan Institute of Performing Arts. Norbu is best known for his polemical writings. The first collection of his political essays, *Illusion and Reality,* was published in 1989. A second collection, *Shadow Tibet,* is to be released in 2005.

Norbu has also written a number of plays as well as a traditional Tibetan opera libretto. He served as a director of the Tibetan Centre for Advanced Studies (the Amnye Machen Institute), which was twice awarded the Poul Lauretzen Freedom Prize of Denmark.

Norbu is a former member of the Tibetan resistance movement in Mustang on the Nepal-Tibet border. He currently lives in Tennessee with his wife and two daughters.